$TEALING YOU BLIND TRICKS OF THE FRAUD TRADE

SNEAKY THEFTS BY CLEVER INDIVIDUALS
A BOOK ON FRAUDS, CONS, AND SCAMS

BY

DETECTIVE K. A. FARNER, ret.

iUniverse, Inc.
New York   Bloomington

Stealing You Blind
Tricks of the Fraud Trade

The information, ideas, and suggestions in this book are not intended to render professional advice. Before following any suggestions contained in this book, you should consult your personal accountant or other financial advisor. Neither the author nor the publisher shall be liable or responsible for any loss or damage allegedly arising as a consequence of your use or application of any information or suggestions in this book. The views expressed in this work are solely those of the author and do not necessarily reflect the views of the publisher, and the publisher hereby disclaims any responsibility for them.

iUniverse books may be ordered through booksellers or by contacting:

iUniverse
1663 Liberty Drive
Bloomington, IN 47403
www.iuniverse.com
1-800-Authors (1-800-288-4677)

Because of the dynamic nature of the Internet, any Web addresses or links contained in this book may have changed since publication and may no longer be valid.

ISBN: 978-1-4401-3953-6 (pbk)
ISBN: 978-1-4401-3952-9 (cloth)
ISBN: 978-1-4401-3954-3 (ebk)

Library of Congress Control Number: 2009926810

Printed in the United States of America

iUniverse rev. date: 4/16/2009

PREFACE

This book is derived from actual police investigations. These incidents describe many of the current fraud trends currently plaguing our society. Many fraudulent schemes and scams use the same general methods however some fraud perpetrators will add new and inventive ideas to their approach to fool unsuspecting and unaware people. Some fraudulent schemes and scams resurface every few years with their methods intact and fool those individuals who do not have any knowledge of their previous existence. Other types of fraudulent crimes will occur just because the fraud perpetrator takes advantage of the way a citizen makes their way through everyday life. The fraud perpetrator has quickly learned that by obtaining public information and using methods to obtain private information, he or she can receive a profit far greater than most other crimes.

First and foremost, fraudulent criminal activity is occurring at an alarming rate in the United States of America. Every few seconds, of every day, a person will become a victim of some type of fraudulent crime. The scary part is that some fraudulent criminal acts cannot be prevented. With such fraudulent criminal acts, a person can only hope that he or she is able to discover the crime quickly, cut his or her loss and/or losses, and minimize the headaches associated with the stress derived from such crimes.

This book was written to inform the general public of some of the fraudulent criminal acts, schemes, and scams which are currently taking place in everyday society and throughout our country. It will not teach people how to commit such crimes or teach those the methods of a law enforcement investigation to identify and apprehend such criminals. It is solely written for the purpose of informing the public of what they now face in everyday life and armed with that knowledge; they can perhaps prevent or deter some type of fraudulent crime in the future.

It is your name, your money, your credit, and your time that is at stake. In the game of fraud, your best defense is knowledge. To quote Ben Franklin

Detective K. A. Farner

"An ounce of prevention is worth a pound of cure." This is especially true with fraudulent criminal acts.

This book is dedicated to my family and my friends.

Contents

Chapter One

Fraudulent Crimes

This book is not intended to make the fraud perpetrator a better criminal or to teach those the methods of a law enforcement investigation. The fraudulent activities mentioned in the following chapters are well known among the majority of con men, scam artists, and fraud perpetrators. According to the Federal Trade Commission or FTC, in excess of 30 million people in the United States in 2007 were victimized by some type of fraudulent criminal incident. If a person takes in to account other related incidents such as counterfeit check fraud and credit card fraud, for example, the number of victims in the United States in astonishing. Each year, more and more people fall victim to these perpetrators. This book was written to inform the general public some of the fraudulent activities, scams, and cons that are present in our every day society. I have always believed that when people are knowledgeable about certain crimes, the less susceptible they are to becoming a victim of one.

The fraud perpetrator uses several different factors to his or her advantage. For the most part, he or she is an actor of deception. Fraud can be explained as stealing by use of deceptive means. In the case of identity fraud, the fraud perpetrator will pretend to be someone else using the victim's personal and financial information to obtain credit, merchandise, and services. The scam artist or con man will often pretend to be someone such as an executive or owner of a business, banker, lawyer, or investment broker when, in fact, he is just playing the part to deceive you of your money. At other times, though, the suspect can be employed in a professional setting and, for one reason or another, decides to defraud others through the use of deceptive means.

Fraudulent criminal acts often require the element of secrecy. With this, the fraud perpetrator can go on deceiving others before the con, scam, or scheme will not work. Credit card fraud, for example, is only successful when the victims are unaware of the fraud. Once the card or card number has been discovered as having been compromised and reported as stolen, the suspects know that he or she cannot use the card for merchandise and/or services. This is why most perpetrators will immediately use a stolen credit card after a theft. This criminal also knows that his or her chance of being detected and arrested increase with time. Fraud suspects might work a particular scam in one area for a short time and then pick up and move somewhere else to work the same exact scam. At other times, knowledge of working scams and cons are passed between perpetrators in different parts of the nation. Some types of fraudulent activity will be re-invented after a period of time when people have let the guard down.

Claims have been made that you can prevent fraudulent criminal acts such as identity fraud but the truth is that it cannot be prevented. Your personal information as well as your financial information can be obtained by these perpetrators even if you take every precaution. The information is available and the fraud perpetrator armed with the right resources can and will find the weak link in the system. I do believe that a person can deter a lot of criminal behavior and even limit the amount of losses and headaches associated with these fraudulent criminal acts when they do become victimized. By knowing what frauds, cons, and scams that perpetrators have committed in the past and present, a person gains the knowledge needed to recognize these for what they are.

These criminal activities have been around for a very long time. Swindlers, con artists, and cheats have been in existence ever since the invention of currency. There are those in each society and within each period of time who prey upon others. In the late twentieth century and now in the twenty-first century, these crimes have increased dramatically. Fraudulent related criminal activities and incidents probably occur as much as all of the other crimes combined. These crimes are far less likely to be reported than most other types of crimes. This may be true because the victim feels that it often more of a hassle to report the incident or perhaps the victim does not want the incident known to anyone. Some businesses will only report a small percentage of crime and will keep the investigation "in house", so to speak. The actual number of fraud related incidents is constantly on the rise and the true amount of these incidents throughout the United States remains unknown and can only be estimated. Fraud related criminal statistics are now gathering much more attention than the same statistics from 10 years ago. Law enforcement and the general public have a better understanding of fraud related criminal acts and as a result of these statistics, law enforcement should be able to direct their manpower to combat these activities.

Chapter Two

The Fraud Perpetrator

Throughout the entire world, there are people that will go to great means to steal money, jewelry, merchandise, and anything else of value from people and businesses. For some of these fraud perpetrators, con men, and scam artists it is their primary source of income. Most people are taught from birth that hard work, education, and financial diligence can lead to a successful career and life. Some people, however, will always attempt to find shortcuts to this success and some will turn to a life of crime. I have made arrests or assisted in the arrest of individuals charged with just about every major crime from murder, rape, burglary, robbery, and thefts or larcenies. Perhaps the most intriguing characters though are the fraud perpetrators. For the most part, they are very imaginative, clever, and sneaky individuals.

So, just who is the fraud perpetrator, confidence person or con man, and scam artist? They come from all walks of life, just like everyone else. The fraud perpetrator, con man, and/or scam artist can be of any color, any religion, any nationality, male or female, and young or old. We have seen men as well as women commit very serious fraudulent crimes as well as teenagers to elderly people. These individuals can be found in every country on every continent. They come from low income families, middle income families, and even well to do families.

Questions always arise as to how the fraud perpetrator came to steal. I suppose that question will never truly be answered or at least not answered in a simple manner. Science has forever attempted to answer questions regarding human behavior such as depression, anger, happiness, etc. The same is true in regards to criminal behavior. Science as well as law enforcement have discovered a lot concerning criminal behavior however no one can predict with any amount of certainty who will become a murderer, rapist, or any other type of criminal including the fraud perpetrator or con man.

The fraud perpetrator or con man often plays the part of someone else. I guess one could refer to these perpetrators as actors or actresses portraying a scene in everyday modern life. We have witnessed several fraud perpetrators that were so efficient with their lies and schemes that they have been able to fool countless people with little or no effort involved. People committing such crimes have portrayed themselves as lawyers, doctors, business men, bankers, investment brokers, real estate brokers, and automobile brokers. Many of the fraud perpetrators we have arrested in the Atlanta area often refer to their crimes as "stunts". The bigger and better the stunt, the more satisfaction the suspect derives from the crime as well as gaining popularity within his or her peer groups. For some fraud perpetrators, it is not simply for monetary gain it is the satisfaction they derive from the "game".

To give you an example of how some modern day fraud perpetrators are extremely imaginative and creative in their "stunts" or criminal acts is one case that a good friend and fellow fraud detective had investigated. The suspect(s) had obtained the financial identifiers of a business and began to fabricate counterfeit checks which were posted to the business' checking account. The manager discovered the thefts and reported the counterfeit check fraud to the major fraud office. The manager acquired copies of the counterfeit checks and presented them, as evidence, to the lead detective. As the lead detective and I were discussing the case, we discovered an interesting fact. All of the checks had the signatures of several former Presidents of the United States on the face of the check. The suspect(s) were able to download the signatures and then imprint the signatures on the counterfeit checks. With each counterfeit check, the fraud perpetrator(s) obtained money or merchandise but, in their own weird minds, were able to pull off a fantastic "stunt" worth bragging about to their fellow fraud criminals.

Throughout history there have always been people who have stolen from others but it seems that in today's world, the number of people who steal is ever on the increase. In many ways, society has begun to accept this type of behavior and in many ways glorified the criminal who committed the criminal act. Every day on every news channel, there is usually a story or two concerning these particular criminal incidents. Hollywood has made numerous movies depicting the life of a criminal as being exciting and lucrative.

Children learn from several different factors in their life, their parents, their friends, their school, their neighborhoods, etc. Every young child has to be taught that certain things such as stealing are incorrect and improper. Too often, however, children from poor neighborhoods will see another person from the same area driving the nice new vehicle, wearing nice clothes, and having lots of spending money which they obtained from illegal means. All too often the child receives the message that, they too, can have the same material things and possessions without working hard and without the benefit of an education. Sometimes, parents fail in teaching their children right from wrong but sometimes it is the other factors that will bring a child or young adult to the other side.

One of the most obvious factors today in the increase of criminal activity involving thefts and fraud is the way the current court system views this type of criminal. All too often, the fraud perpetrator is given many chances to give up on this type of behavior and conduct an honest living. It may take several convictions in a court of law before the fraud perpetrator is actually given any jail time. The court system has a tremendous job of attempting to balance justice in the ever increasing population of the jails and prisons. Violent crimes committed by people convicted of such crimes carry a higher rate of incarceration than those crimes committed by people which for the most part were nonviolent. Not very many people would disagree that a violent offender such a murderer, a rapist, child molester, or an armed robber should receive jail time over a person who committed a non-violent crime. The problem arises because we, as a nation, are currently over run with people convicted of all types of crimes and only a small amount of jail and prison space is available. Jurisdictions have even been fined because of housing too many inmates as was the case of Fulton County a few years ago. For this reason, many fraud perpetrators are given probation or community service.

The lack of punishment for the average fraud perpetrator is not only known in the law enforcement community but also known by the majority of such criminals. This is just one reason why people who would not normally commit such a crime do commit the crime. Some are willing to take the risk involved because that they know if they are captured, one night in jail will be the extent of his or her punishment. The following day, the fraud perpetrator is usually given bond and released with a court date pending. Unless the individual has an extremely long RAP or record of arrest and prosecution sheet or has committed the fraud with heinous circumstances, they will probably not see much actual jail time. This type of revolving door will keep a person committing fraud and actually helps other perpetrators to recruit new members to commit fraudulent acts for them.

No doubt, it is a very tough and difficult situation. The United States of America has a limited amount of jail space for people who are convicted of crimes and the overall number of fraudulent crimes is on the increase each and every year. Some say that building more and larger jails and prisons would eliminate a lot of repeat offenders from victimizing new victims. I agree to some extent; however, jails and prisons cost a lot of money to build and maintain.

Today's fraud perpetrator is very different from the fraud perpetrator of years gone by. He or she finds it relatively easy to find a victim, either a person or a business, for his or her criminal act. This person does not have to have the knowledge of machines such as printing presses as the fraud perpetrator of years past, they only need the knowledge of a computer and high tech printer in many cases. Our current technological age has enabled the fraud perpetrator to obtain public information and to obtain private or confidential information of individuals and businesses alike. If the fraud perpetrator does not have the knowledge to obtain the information, he or she quickly find the resources which will teach them. Because this information is readily obtained by criminals, I strongly recommend that every person and every business prepare a good defense against fraudulent activity.

Another thing to consider regarding a lot of fraud related crimes is the drug nexus or drug connection. In recent years, we have observed that many fraud perpetrators either use or deal in illegal narcotics especially crystal methamphetamine or ICE. A lot of fraud perpetrators will facilitate illegal narcotics with fraudulent criminal acts. For the most part, the fraud suspect will obtain money and merchandise whenever and wherever he or she can and will use these to purchase illegal narcotics. Unfortunately, major drug dealers do exist in just about every city and town in the nation and will continue to exist as long as there is supply and demand for the illegal narcotic. Law enforcement has seen an increase in the number of people who use illegal narcotics and fraud related crimes. I suppose this may be a vicious circle of the life of a person addicted to illegal drugs. People addicted to illegal drugs often find it very difficult to hold down any type of legitimate work. Therefore, they turn to whatever means to obtain their illegal narcotics which usually means that they turn to stealing. This addiction will lead the addict to steal from their parents, siblings, friends, and anyone else.

Most companies and businesses now deploy some type of background check regarding criminal histories and credit histories because of the increase in drug use, thefts, and fraudulent activity over the years. Some businesses even require their employees to undergo drug testing on a regular basis. Often, businesses will not hire an employee if he or she has been convicted of a theft related crime or has had a history of drug use or a conviction for drug possession. For all of the people who might consider committing a fraudulent crime, you might want to reconsider because if you are caught, the arrest might follow you around for the rest of your life. It could possibly ruin any chances that you might have on landing that dream job several years down the road.

Chapter Three

Scams

The experienced con man or confidence man can and will perpetrate just about anything if it involves money. The con man or scam artist can be male or female, young or old, and can be of any race. All shapes and sizes. The basic principal of any confidence game is to find a willing subject to be their victim. This victim has to believe in what the scam artist is selling or doing. Often the scam artist will prey upon their victims' good nature. This can be accomplished by pretending to be handicapped, pretending to be some type of disaster relief after a natural disaster or any other disaster.

We had an ongoing problem in Atlanta with juvenile fraud suspects. These juveniles would go to the local malls or shopping centers and approach the victims as they were either entering or exiting the malls. These individuals were between eight years old to fourteen years old. They would draw up some type of paper explaining that their football, basketball, or baseball team was raising funds to go to camp. The juveniles would ask each person for a donation so that the juvenile and his friends could attend the camp. They were friendly, courteous, and dressed in nice jeans and a shirt. Although there would often be four or five people running this scam together, they were smart enough not to approach a potential victim with the entire group. This would often alarm or scare the victim. Their approach was subtle with one or perhaps two juveniles approaching the potential victim so as not to scare the victims. They also knew not to scare the potential victim by startling them, so they would wait until the victim had a clear view of them approaching before they made contact.

Not everyone would give money to the young suspects. But it was surprising as to how many people did give them money. The donations would be anywhere between one dollar up to twenty dollars. By the end of the day, after approaching hundreds of citizens, they walked away with hundreds of dollars in their pockets. These little guys were quickly learning how to deceive others and that the deception could be quite rewarding. Victims, who had given these young fraud perpetrators money, believed that the kids were obtaining money to go to the camps and they wanted to help them achieve that goal. Going to a basketball, baseball, or football camp or any other school activity is a great thing for any child, if the camp actually exists. In these cases, it did not and the kids were obtaining money from good natured citizens based on a lie. Fund raising events are necessary; however, they should be done in an honest, legal manner. First, if these children were raising money for camp, a teacher or coach should have been there also. Before giving any donation, a citizen should verify that the organization or team actually exists and gather information that can either prove the children's claims or shed light on a scam.

The second type of scam is quite common in Atlanta and every major city in America that has a homeless population. Now, I am not downgrading a person's right to do whatever he or she wants to do. We are a free nation and people can choose, whether consciously or subconsciously, to be anything he or she wants to be and to live how they want. I am not knocking homeless people mind you, only those take advantage of another human being. Everyone needs and deserves a little help now and then and there are organizations, agencies, and churches that will assist those that are down on their luck, so to speak, to get back on their feet. I am speaking about the person standing at an intersection or interstate exit ramp of a busy roadway begging others for money. In Atlanta, we had several individuals who would do this each and every day. One person, in particular, had been arrested so many times almost every officer knew his name. At the time of each and every arrest, this guy always had between $300 to $500 dollars on his person. He would obtain this money, in a few hours, standing in a busy intersection. It was all a farce. Good natured people were giving this guy and others like him their hard earned money so that he could buy something to eat. The problem, however, was that this was an every day occurrence and he would obtain in a day of begging what many of the people who had given him some money would spend on food in a month. You might ask where the money went after this guy obtained it, mostly it went for drugs and alcohol.

Another scam of some of these guys is to pretend to be a person who cannot speak and cannot hear. These guys will write on a crumpled up piece of paper that they are deaf, mute, homeless, and haven't eaten in several days. They approach citizens giving them the piece of paper and the good hearted citizen will open up their wallet or purse to these guys. Most of the time, an officer responding to complaints of such a person will feel the same feelings of sorrow and just have the person move on.

I had the experience of one such gentleman at a professional sporting event. I don't know if the guy had gotten enough money to purchase a ticket to the event or if someone had just given him one. In any case, he was allowed to enter the stadium with the rest of the spectators. Once inside the stadium, he began to approach people with families begging for money. A lot of citizens complained that he was becoming a nuisance and that his body odor was offending. Stadium officials wanted him removed from the premises and the subject left. A few games later, he was back doing the same thing and once again spectators began to complain. This time an officer took his information and the management issued him a criminal trespass warning before escorting him from the property. If he returned to the property within a period of one year, he could be arrested for criminal trespass.

Within one week, he was back. He probably would have gotten away with coming back but, as before, he began to bother other spectators and they complained to the management. The subject became belligerent and was arrested for criminal trespass. As I was processing the individual and waiting on the wagon to transport him to jail, the suspect asked me if he could smoke a cigarette. I told him that no cigarettes were allowed inside of the building however I would take him outside and let him smoke while we waited on the wagon. He said thanks and we struck up a conversation while waiting for the wagon. All of this time, he had everyone fooled into thinking that he could not hear or speak, everyone including me. This guy really could play the part well. It just goes to show that not everything is as it appears.

Scam artists can victimize businesses also. One business that the scam artist will hit will be that of large four star or five star hotels. In one case that I investigated, the scam artist called the hotel, in advance, claiming that he was a celebrity traveling from Los Angeles and he needed a room for two or three days. The celebrity's name that the suspect used did make a lot of trips to the Atlanta area and had stayed at the hotel previously. The fraud suspect, after making the reservation, requested to be transferred to the billing department. After a few moments, he called the front desk back and told them that everything had been arranged and would they please leave the hotel room key at the front desk in an envelope. He told the front desk clerk that he would be arriving late that night and would have an assistant pick up the hotel room key for him. The suspect arrived that night and picked up the key. He spent the night in the hotel room and then skipped out the following morning without paying.

The second of such cases was a bit more complicated and the suspect was well acquainted with how hotels conduct business. The suspect telephoned a four star hotel in Atlanta and requested a line of credit for his company. The hotel clerk then transferred him to the accounts department. He explained to the accounts clerk that he was the Chief Executive Officer of a telecommunication business located in Ohio and his company was in the process of opening another branch office in Atlanta. He requested a credit application for a line of credit be faxed to him at his office. The accounts clerk immediately faxed a copy to the suspect. The fraud perpetrator then completed the application with bogus information regarding his bank accounts and creditors. After completing the line of credit application, he faxed the application back to the accounts clerk and telephoned her to inform her to expect the fax. The clerk received the fax and began to check the references of the suspect. Using a trick that counterfeit check fraud perpetrators commonly use, this individual had listed several cellular telephone numbers as the phone numbers of the bank and other creditors. These cellular telephones belonged to the suspect or his accomplices. When the clerk checked the references, she called the numbers on the application. When one of the cellular phones would ring, the perpetrator knew and had someone answer the telephone with the greeting of the particular business he had listed. As the clerk would inquire about the suspect, an acquaintance of the suspect would give him an "A" rating. When the clerk had telephoned all of the listed references, he was approved for the line of credit.

After receiving the line of credit, the suspect arrived at the hotel a few days later and stayed at the hotel for approximately twenty days amassing quite a hotel and room service bill. The individual then checked out of the hotel and the hotel sent him a bill the following week. Because part of the suspect's stay at the hotel came in one billing cycle and the other part of the stay came in another billing cycle, the first bill was a little over a thousand dollars. After about three weeks after receiving the first bill, the perpetrator had not remitted any payment.

This particular hotel had a special promotion at the time of the scam; they were giving one free night for every four nights that a person stayed at the hotel. Since the suspect had stayed at the hotel for more that twenty days, he had been awarded five free stays at the hotel. A little over four weeks had expired since the suspect had checked out of the hotel and he was back with his family to redeem the five free nights. The hotel's manager, at this time, began to smell a rat. He knew that this person had stayed at the hotel previously and knew that he had an extremely large outstanding balance which he had not made any payments. The hotel manager and the hotel's security director detained the suspect, began to question him, and called the police. He was questioned at that time and then released because we could not, at that specific time, prove any fraud. It was late at night and it was impossible to verify or contradict anything on the application. We could not make an arrest before verifying that a crime had been committed. At the time, we did not have enough Probable Cause to exact an arrest. After the suspect left the premises, an investigation commenced.

A few weeks later, evidence had been obtained proving that the suspect had submitted a fraudulent application and arrest warrants for his arrest were obtained. It is sad that the victim had to wait for justice but it is far better for everyone to first verify and confirm that a crime had taken place before exacting any arrest. Jurisdictions as well as businesses have jumped the gun on a few cases in the past and it has cost them dearly. Mere suspicion that someone has committed a criminal act is never enough. All law enforcement officers must adhere to the Fourth Amendment of the Bill of Rights.

Scam artists will also take advantage of good natured people in times when disaster strikes. Such was the case with Hurricane Katrina and other natural disasters that have occurred in the United States in recent years. Always be mindful of who you are sending your donations to, be sure to check out the charity or organization first. It should be registered to accept donations from people. If, after researching the business, you find that it is legitimate by all means make the donation. If, after researching the business, you find no record of the business I would not recommend making the donation until you can verify the charity or organization.

Chapter Four

Schemes

There are a lot of schemes in the world today. Some have been around for over a hundred years. Some schemes are new versions with added twists of the original plot invented long ago. These criminal acts can range in the victim loosing as little as $1.00 to an advanced Ponzi scheme were the loss could be in the millions of dollars.

I have been involved in a couple of investigations which would be considered Ponzi schemes. The scheme itself was named after a swindler by the name of Ponzi. Ponzi offered investors, in the early part of the twentieth century, huge returns on their initial investments within a very short period of time. Initial investors in the criminal enterprise will usually receive their investment plus a large profit. This is done as more and more investors join the scheme. The money derived from the latter investors is used to pay the initial investors. Some of the initial investors, at this point, will re-invest their funds back into the scheme. Investors are often given fraudulent financial reports which state their investment has grown. Fraud perpetrators using the Ponzi scheme will often offer something of value to their potential victims such as real estate, vehicles, stocks, bonds, etc. As long as the investors keep investing, the plot will continue. In the majority of Ponzi schemes, the fraud perpetrator(s) will not invest the investor's funds as promised but use the funds for their own personal use. When the scheme begins to fall apart, the fraud perpetrator will attempt to take the remaining funds and disappear.

Ponzi schemes are often difficult to investigate because they usually involve a number of people and a lot of money. Attorneys, for the defendants, in Ponzi schemes will often argue that it is a civil matter, just bad business and criminal acts were not committed. The defense will always show people who profited from the investment scheme to contradict those that lost money.

The bottom line is that stealing is stealing whether the victim's number one or they number in the thousands. Taking funds from an individual meant for investment and then using those funds for the personal gain or personal use of the person receiving these investments is a theft, no matter how you look at it.

Several years back, I had several friends who had been scammed by fraud perpetrators running a pyramid scheme. A pyramid scheme can be known by several different aliases but just about all have the same method of operation. Unlike the Ponzi scheme, the pyramid scheme is based upon the participation of recruits and involves only the investment of their money for the opportunity to receive other recruit's investments. An individual or group of individuals can start a pyramid scheme. The individual or group will then recruit others explaining that they can receive a tremendous return on their initial investment. The new recruit is required to invest his or her money which can be anywhere from $100 to $1000 or more. The recruit is told how the process works and for them to get their money back, several other new recruits are needed. As more and more new recruits are added to the pyramid, the person at the top of the pyramid drops off and the second person in line takes the top position. After enough people have been recruited again, this new number one man gets his money. The initial third man in the pyramid then takes the primary spot and the process is done again. This will continue until the pyramid cannot find any more new recruits or law enforcement steps in and arrests those involved. In schemes like these, the fraud perpetrators will make money and then exit. A few recruits might make money but about 9 out of 10 loose their investment. Never get caught up in this because, one it is illegal, and two, it is immoral. Individuals who participate in a pyramid scheme are what I would refer to as being not an innocent victim. Participants are gambling that other people will also gamble and if they do, money can be made. Nothing is bought or sold. It is simply one person taking money from several other people. People involved with this scheme are as guilty as those who created it.

Another type of scheme is the chain letter. The chain letter scheme was very popular several years ago and different versions still exist to this day. A person receives a letter which usually contains a brief message regarding how you can make money and a list of names and addresses. The chain letter advises you to send a certain amount of currency to the first person named in the letter. The amounts can vary between $1.00 to $10.00 and more. The person is then advised to cross out that person's name and address and to place their name and address at the bottom of the list of names. The person is then instructed to mail these to as many people as possible. The more letters mailed, the greater the return. The letters usually requested $1.00 but others have requested more. I have known several people who had participated in this type of scheme; some actually made money while others lost theirs. Chain letters usually will contain some bogus warning which will read, something to the effect of, if a person breaks the chain, bad luck will be bestowed upon them or by keeping the chain going, the person will receive good luck. The chain letter of this type is illegal and does constitute mail fraud. Once again, the bottom line is that people are taking advantage of others. Some people will make a lot of money, some will make some money, some will break even, and then everyone else will lose their money.

Have you ever looked in the classified section of a newspaper and saw an advertisement for something like this? Earn $1000 a day or week stuffing envelopes from home, call xxx-xxx-xxxx. A lot of people would love to have the opportunity to earn extra cash especially if it is from their own home. People will answer ads such as these and are advised that to begin, they must purchase supplies or pay an initiation fee. A few weeks after purchasing the supplies, the person will receive a package in the mail. The package may contain some type of advertisement for the sale of some small type of merchandise which you could find at any dollar store, an advertisement to make money stuffing envelopes, envelopes, and a mailing list containing names and addresses. Not exactly what the person had in mind. Most think that they will get paid for placing letters or advertisements inside of the envelopes and they will be paid for each letter that they stuff. But this is not the case. The person just received about $2.00 in envelopes with an advertisement and mailing list which is a far cry from their initial investment. The person is then instructed to mail the advertisements to people on the mailing list. The person is told that earnings will be based on the actual replies to these letters. Actually, this particular scheme is related to the pyramid scheme only these schemes use the guise of an actual business. As more victims are acquired and numerous letters mailed, more money is made for the fraud suspect(s). Legitimate businesses, on the other hand, will offer merchandise or services which will or can be marketed at a fair price. Their prices will be in line with other legitimate products and services. The business which is based on a scheme might promise to provide products or services but these products and/or services are not worth what the victim has paid for them. These companies will make claims of making money; however in most, the victim will lose money. During hard times or when the economy is struggling, work at home schemes become more prominent. Be very careful before ever committing to anything without doing some research first.

Remember, good things usually take a lot of time, hard work, and commitment. If you are thinking about entering a business venture, do a lot of research first. Check with private firms such as the Better Business Bureau, state agencies, and federal agencies regarding the business. If the business has been in business a long time, some agency will have some records. If the business is relatively new or a start up, there will not be any records available. In new business ventures, research as much as possible and take your time. Before ever giving any money to the venture, make sure what you are purchasing is actually worth what you will be paying.

Chapter Five

Identity Fraud

Anyone at anytime can become a victim of identity fraud or identity theft. Even if you take every precaution, the identity fraud perpetrator can steal your information. They can obtain these records by actually entering a business and stealing the information, through a dishonest employee who smuggles the information for a fee, by accessing a particular database and downloading the files which contain your information, a fraudulent email, dumpster diving through your garbage, dumpster diving at a business that did not protect your records as they should had, and even steal your information from your own residence. To make matters worse, between one quarter and one third of all identity fraud suspects are someone the victim knows very well and could even be a relative of the victim. A person can become a victim of identity fraud anytime anyone uses any part of their personal information or financial information without permission or authorization.

I have always used the term identity fraud whenever speaking of the crimes committed by fraud perpetrators who commit such crimes by using someone else's personal or financial identifiers. Many publications, organizations, and laws will refer to the crimes committed by these perpetrators as identity theft. Whenever I arrested a subject for this type of criminal act, the charge was written according to the state's code which was labeled as identity theft. I have often used fraud to describe the actual use of someone's information and theft to describe the possession of someone's information. Criminal acts concerning financial transaction cards or numbers, for example, have two primary charges in the state of Georgia. One is the mere possession of someone's financial card or number and the other is the actual use of the financial card or number by the perpetrator. In the first, the charge is financial transaction card theft and with the latter, the charge is financial transaction card fraud. The same is true to describe the difference between forgery in the first degree and forgery in the second degree. The two charges are almost identical; however, forgery in the first degree is defined as the actual uttering or passing of the forged instrument while forgery in the second degree meant the mere possession of the counterfeit instrument.

Identity fraud is a billion dollar business for the fraud perpetrator. Victims, that have spent an entire lifetime building a respectable credit history, are now faced with the problems of having their credit destroyed and the problems associated with attempting to correct those problems. Victims of identity fraud will spend countless hours and money attempting to correct the problems created by the identity fraud perpetrator. In some cases, the victim has been faced with civil suits, garnishment of their wages, and even criminal charges.

Without a doubt, identity theft or identity fraud is the fastest growing crime in the United States of America. It is damaging the very fiber of our lives and removing trust from the equation in the Free Enterprise system. Modern day financing has made it possible for just about everyone to obtain loans or some type of credit to purchase things a lot easier. Today, most businesses offer loans, lines of credit, and credit cards to anyone with a credit score which will reflect that the person is a good candidate for repaying the loan, line of credit, or credit card. The identity fraud suspect is quickly ruining this for others.

Identity fraud can, at times, become a nightmare for the victim and also a very difficult case for the detective to solve. The victim may not discover that he or she has become a victim for several months after the initial fraud occurred. Usually this discovery comes at the hand of some collection agency or business contacting them because of an overdue bill. The victim then might discover more fraud after that and spend numerous months or even years attempting to prove to the creditors that they had not made the charges or purchases before finally having the creditor remove the information from their credit report. Once a company reports a bad debt or collection account to the three major credit reporting agencies, that same company is the only party that can request that the bad debt or collection be removed from your account. If the victim is unable to convince the company or business that they are a victim of an identity fraud, the victim may be forced to bring a civil proceeding against that company or business just to clear his or her name and have the fraudulent debts removed from their credit history. All of this process can be an extremely stressful and frustrating period for the victim. Citizens can dispute anything on their credit history and, by law, all falsehoods including identity fraud must be removed. Simply disputing the account will not always lead to the account being removed from a person's credit history.

By filing a dispute, the credit reporting agency contacts the business that owns the account and an investigation into the dispute should be conducted by that business. If the business does not agree with your dispute, it may take the action of an attorney to have the case settled.

I worked a case of identity fraud involving the victim's personal identifiers, name, date of birth, social security number, etc, which was used by a suspect each and every time the suspect received medical treatment. The suspect and the victim each had the same first name and the same last name but had different middle names, dates of births, and social security numbers. Both of the victims had received treatment from the same medical facility at one time. It is suspected that the suspect obtained the victim's information through a medical file or statement that had erroneously been given to her. After receiving this information, the suspect began to receive treatment at several medical centers using the victim's information. The suspect was suffering from a terminal illness and the medical bills from this treatment began to amount. The victim began to receive bills for the medical treatment and immediately filed a police report and fraud affidavits with each of the collection agencies and medical facilities. Thinking that this had solved her problem, the victim continued on with her everyday life. Not long after filing the police reports and mailing the fraud affidavits, the calls and letters from collection agencies started again insisting that she pay the outstanding medical bills or face a civil suit. The victim told each collection agent again that she was a victim of identity fraud but it fell upon deaf ears. She continued to receive harassing telephone calls and letters from the collection agencies.

Up to this point, the victim's report had not been investigated. The Major Fraud Unit had four detectives and each detective had an extremely large caseload. Fraud cases can be time consuming and require the detective to exhaust an extensive amount of work on each case. One lead can easily magnify into ten leads and one suspect can quickly grow to ten suspects. Simply speaking, the detectives of the Major Fraud Unit, at that time, were assigned those cases however it was impossible for them to work that many. The other fraud detectives and I worked as many cases as we could but we could not work all that were assigned. In the beginning, this particular case was not being worked.

The victim began to investigate on her own and discovered that the suspect had also applied for an apartment lease using the victim's personal identifiers. The victim drove to the apartment complex and requested a copy of the application. The apartment complex agreed because the information contained upon the application was that of the victim's. As the victim reviewed the application, she noticed that the suspect had listed the name and telephone number of a possible relative of the suspect as a reference. The victim then called the telephone number and spoke with the wife of the person listed as a reference. This person explained that the suspect was her mother-in-law and that she was suffering from a terminal illness. The daughter-in-law also told the victim that the suspect had a history of fraudulent crimes and drug abuse. After this discussion, the daughter-in-law and the son met with the victim and decided to come down to the Major Fraud office and speak with a detective. It just so happened, that I was the detective on office duty that particular day. As I listened to the victim and all of the problems that this suspect had caused her and to the son and daughter-in-law who were trying to live an honest life and had attempted to get the suspect help, I decided that this case needed immediate attention. I gathered statements and evidence on the case, eventually gaining enough Probable Cause, to obtain an arrest warrant for the suspect. Before she was arrested for the crimes though, the suspect passed away from her terminal illness.

The victim continued to receive calls and letters from collection agents regarding the outstanding medical bills even though the case had been cleared. The victim came to the Major Fraud office one day and she was crying. She asked if I could help her with the collection agencies that were harassing her and I agreed. I made a telephone call to one collection agency in Nashville, Tennessee and spoke to the collection agent. I explained the case to the collection agent and asked her if she had received the affidavits that the victim had sent her. The collection agent replied that she did not have any faith in affidavits and, frankly, did not believe in them. I advised the collection agent that, especially in this case, that she should start. I advised the victim of her legal rights and suggested that she file a complaint with the Federal Trade Commission regarding the collection agency.

The Federal Trade Commission receives more complaints regarding collection agencies than any other type of business. In recent years, it has become common place for a lot of businesses to sell off their old and expired accounts which, for one reason or another, had defaulted. These are accounts which the business has written off as a loss. Certain businesses will purchase these accounts for pennies on the dollar or perhaps purchase a debt of thousands for just a few cents. Although the unpaid debt might have occurred several years earlier in the person's life and has since been removed from their personal credit history, the new owner of these debts, the collection agency, will attempt to collect the debt from the individual. If the collection agency is successful in collecting even a partial amount of the outstanding debt, their profit is enormous. No doubt, the identity fraud perpetrator's accounts will be some of those accounts which are purchased and the identity fraud victim will have to relive the nightmare again years later.

Years ago, while a patrol officer, I received a call to respond to an area home improvement store on a shoplifting call. Upon my arrival at the location, I was met by the store's loss prevention manager who replied that he had observed a male take several items of merchandise from the store's shelves, place them inside of his clothing, and then exit the business without paying for the items. The loss prevention manager detained the individual outside of the store, relocated him to the loss prevention office, and then notified the police. After hearing the loss prevention manager's statement and obtaining the business' wish to prosecute the individual for the crime, I placed the suspect under arrest and the advised him of his Constitutional Rights. The suspect stated that he wanted to cut a deal and he had information regarding a fencing operation but he would only speak to a detective. I contacted detective radio and spoke with the detective sergeant who replied that no one was available, at the time, to respond. The suspect heard this conversation and stated that he would not speak with me but only a detective.

The suspect did not have any form of identification upon his person so I began to obtain the information from him verbally. He stated his name, date of birth, and social security number. I then proceeded to check the suspect for wants and/or warrants on tactical radio. Tactical radio advised me that the suspect had a valid Georgia driver's license and did not have any wants and/or warrants. My gut instinct told me differently. I requested tactical radio give me a description of the suspect. Tactical radio advised that the description was 6 feet 1 inch and had a weight of 240 pounds. The suspect, in front of me, was about 5 feet 7 inches and weighed approximately 170 pounds. He had overheard tactical radio's description and immediately replied that he had lost weight. I then replied that he had shrunk to. I took the suspect to our identification unit to be fingerprinted and attempted to discover his true identity. As luck would have it, nothing came back on the suspect. He was then transported to jail and booked under the name he had given me.

I kept thinking that this guy was not who he claimed to be and that he probably had outstanding warrants for his arrest. I contacted a friend who was a detective and told him about the case. I gave the detective the suspect's information and he went to work attempting to discover the suspect's true identity. After a few hours, the detective notified me that he had discovered the suspect's true identity and for me to meet him at court. It was discovered that the suspect had, indeed, given a false name and date of birth. I was correct about the suspect; he had an outstanding warrant for rape in another state. The suspect was re-identified and then extradited back to the other state to face charges.

Incidents such as the one in the aforementioned paragraphs still occur today as officers and police agencies throughout the United States attempt to identify these suspects for their true identity. Sometimes, the perpetrator will slip through. In the aforementioned case, if this had occurred the suspect would have spent a few days in jail on the shoplifting charge and then be released on a bond with a court date to reappear in court. In this scenario, the suspect would never return to court because his true identity was undiscovered and he would be a long way away. The court, at the date of the suspect's scheduled hearing, would issue a FTA or failure to appear warrant for the suspect's alias name. Since this was a real person with a valid Georgia license and residence, he might have been arrested for the FTA, transported to jail, and had to prove that he was a victim of identity theft. Jurisdictions throughout the United States have since changed the methods of retrieving a fugitive from justice. Many now require that positive identification be made before exacting an arrest. This usually requires the officer or officers comparing the suspect's photograph with the individual that they have in front of them. Still, some people are detained and even arrested because someone else used their personal identifiers to evade police detection.

I attempted to work a case from a lady, in California, that had become an identity fraud victim. Someone had obtained all of her personal information and had opened up several accounts in the Atlanta area. The victim discovered the incident after she received a telephone call from a collection agency regarding a past due balance on one of the fraudulent accounts. When the victim retrieved her credit reports, she discovered that the suspect or suspects had opened up more that one such account. She began to contact each and every business explaining that she was a victim of identity fraud and she sent identity fraud affidavits to each business. The suspects not only opened up charge accounts, in the victim's name, but also opened up a checking account using the victim's information. The victim soon discovered that she could not even write a personal check to any business because her name and account had been flagged as having numerous checks returned for non sufficient funds or was flagged as fraudulent. It took the victim several more months before she could once again write checks.

The initial fraud had occurred almost a year earlier and obtaining any evidence of the crime with the hope of possibly identifying a suspect was almost nonexistent. The suspect had given a vacant house as their residence and no video surveillance existed by the time I began my investigation. I did what I could but all leads had gone stale. The victim had placed a fraud alert on her credit history at the time of her initial discovery that she had become an identity fraud victim but two years later contacted the Major Fraud office reporting that someone was, once again, using her personal information to open up a charge account in Atlanta. The account was not successfully opened but it didn't stop the suspects from attempting to gain access a second time almost two years later.

One day, as I was working my beat, I had stopped at a convenience store to purchase a cup of coffee. After purchasing my coffee, I stepped outside the store onto the sidewalk. As I was standing on the sidewalk of the convenience store drinking my coffee, I noticed a large black male wearing nice casual clothes run from around the rear of the business and through the parking area. The male did not see me and as he ran between the gas pumps, I witnessed him throw something into a trash can. Realizing that this guy had just committed some type of criminal offense, I began to chase the suspect and then detain him. After I had detained the person in question, two loss prevention employees from the home improvement business next to the convenience store came running through the parking area. The two loss prevention employees explained that the suspect had just attempted to open up an instant charge account to purchase thousands of dollars of home improvement items using a stolen identity. The store had been victimized by several similar incidents in the past few months and the loss prevention department was carefully investigating all new credit applications for fraud. After placing the suspect in my patrol vehicle, I walked back to the trash can and looked inside. A brown wallet was laying on top of several pieces of trash. The wallet contained a counterfeit identification card with the suspect's photograph.

The suspect was arrested, returned to the store, and the case was investigated. After placing the individual under arrest, I advised him of his Constitutional Rights. He replied that he understood these Rights and agreed to speak with me concerning the incident. I soon discovered that the suspect had been recruited by several other perpetrators to enter businesses armed with a counterfeit identification card containing the personal information of a victim and then request a line of credit or instant credit so that he or she could purchase merchandise. He said that the main suspects were employed as used car salespeople and that one of the suspects would research the obituaries looking for recently deceased individuals. After obtaining the name and date of birth of the recently deceased person, they would then proceed to obtain the rest of the deceased individual's personal identifiers. Once the suspects had all of the information that he or she needed, a victim's credit report would be obtained. If the credit report revealed a high credit score, the suspects would then manufacture a counterfeit identification card containing most of the victim's information and a photograph of the runner. The runner was then taken to a business, given a list of items he or she was to purchase, and told to apply for instant credit using the deceased victim's information.

These perpetrators did not have any feelings, whatsoever, for the victim or the victim's immediate family. All that they we interested in was obtaining merchandise which could be resold. Dealing with the death of a loved one is often a tragic period for family and friends. During this time, families of the deceased victims do not need to have the added stress of an investigation of a fraudulent offense. Many fraud suspects do not have a conscience whatsoever.

We had a very intriguing case several years ago. Late one afternoon, we received a call from radio dispatch that a stolen vehicle was being chased into our zone. Radio dispatch, at that time, did not know that the stolen vehicle wasn't being chased by any police agency but instead was being tracked by a GPS system. Whenever a large police agency receives a call for service, the call is placed to the 911 operator. The 911 operator will take the call and relay the information into the system. The system will then direct the call to the radio operator of the appropriate zone and dispatch the call to the beat car or, in this case, to all patrol vehicles in the zone. As radio dispatch was receiving this message, units were scrambling attempting to locate the stolen vehicle on the interstate system and roadways. Radio dispatch advised that the vehicle had three occupants and was heading to a restaurant. As I was searching for the vehicle, I wondered how radio knew they were going to a restaurant and that three people were inside of the vehicle. Soon after, radio announced that the vehicle was going inside of an apartment complex in our zone. Units responded to the location and entered the apartment complex. Another officer and I located the vehicle within the complex. It was parked and locked. There were two individuals standing nearby and about to enter another parked vehicle which was parked beside the stolen vehicle. This was also a luxury vehicle which had been recently purchased and still had the dealer's sticker on the glass. These two individuals were detained until we could verify their identity. As we were verifying their identity, we ran a check on both vehicles and both were confirmed as stolen. The two individuals were arrested and advised of their Constitutional Rights.

After securing the two suspects, officers attempted to locate the third suspect but were unsuccessful. It is believed that he resided in the apartment complex and hid in his apartment when officers responded to the scene. As I got back to my patrol vehicle, I began to read the narrative of the call which was quite lengthy. According to the narrative of the 911 call, the three suspects were being tracked by GPS through Atlanta. As the three were traveling through the city, the GPS was able to overhear and record their conversation. Since the vehicle had been stolen from the dealer, the vehicle manufacturer turned the tracking device on and recorded all of the conversations within the vehicle. That is how we discovered that there were three suspects in the vehicle and that they were heading to a restaurant in our zone.

As I continued to read the narrative, I was amazed how much of the conversation had been captured by the GPS. The one male suspect had made a statement to the unknown male suspect stating that, in addition to these two stolen cars, he had two other stolen luxury vehicles parked in his apartment complex. I looked at the suspect's driver's license and saw that his address was in another part of Atlanta. At that time, I called a detective, who was at the scene, over to my car. I knew that he had worked the previous zone as an uniformed patrol officer and he could get someone over to the suspect's apartment complex. The detective called the other zone and units responded to the suspect's apartment complex. Shortly thereafter, we were notified that the two other vehicles had been found and that they had been confirmed as being stolen. Quite a night, we recovered four stolen luxury vehicles worth in excess of $200,000. All of the recovered stolen vehicles had been purchased by the suspect who had used other victims' personal and financial identifiers to obtain financing.

Identity fraud perpetrators can also use your personal information to file fraudulent tax returns with the Internal Revenue Service and receive refund checks in your name before you ever file your legitimate return. The fraud perpetrator will usually open up a bogus account with a banking institution using your personal identifiers and then file a fraudulent return with the I.R.S. Suspects can do this either via U.S. mail or through the internet. They purchase or manufacture counterfeit W2 forms using your personal identifiers which reflect bogus wages and Federal/State withholdings. These fraud perpetrators will receive the refund either by check or direct deposit and immediately cash the refund check or withdraw the funds from the fraudulent account. Victims of this particular type of identity fraud will often file their federal or state tax return only to be informed that another return already exists and to contact their local I.R.S. office or their state's department of revenue office. This presents a very difficult set of problems for the victims of such crimes. The victim has to prove to a large federal or state system, with a limited amount of employees, that they did not file two returns and that they are the victim of identity theft. This procedure can be long and arduous, sometimes taking years to rectify. If the victim is expecting a legitimate refund from their tax return, they will not receive any of the refund until the case of the fraudulent return filed by the fraud perpetrator(s) is proven as fraud. As you can see, preventing this type of fraudulent activity is almost impossible. The best that you can do is safe guard your personal and financial information and make certain that when you do give out such information to a person or business that the person or business is honest and reliable.

Victims can also face criminal charges and even be arrested for the identity fraud suspect's actions and/or crimes. Check fraud committed by the fraud suspect using the victim's name will often begin with the business receiving a check back from a banking institution marked as non sufficient funds or a closed account. The checks written by the fraud suspect are basically a forgery but the business does not know this because the victim is usually unaware of the crimes. After a business receives such a check marked as non sufficient funds, they will turn the check over to their collections department or the company that guarantees the checks, if the business possesses such. Some small businesses prefer to handle matters such as this on their own. Regardless, the business, the business' collection department, or the check guarantor will send a demand letter demanding payment of the check plus a handling fee to the name and address on the returned check. If the suspect has opened up an account using the victim's information but has listed a vacant residence as the address, the victim may not discover the forgery and never receive the business' demand letter. In Georgia and some other states, the business or person receiving a bad check for insufficient funds may proceed with criminal actions after sending a demand letter to the account holder listed on the check. In accordance with state law regarding deposit account fraud, the person or business may commence criminal procedures if the demands of letter are not met within the specified time. Some businesses will turn the case over to their local police department to investigate and others will bypass the investigation and apply for an arrest warrant for the account holder. More than one victim has been forced to appear in court attempting to convince the Judge that it was not he or she that had written such a check.

Other cases have seen the victim's driver's license suspended because of an identity fraud perpetrators actions or violations and still others have been arrested and sent to jail for crimes that they did not commit because someone else used their personal identifiers to deceive law enforcement. For instance, several people have been arrested by jurisdictions serving a bench warrant for a person for a FTA or failure to appear warrant. The suspect had been arrested by a police department or law enforcement agency for a driving violation or criminal offense. The identity fraud suspect will not have any identification on his or her person and will give the arresting officer an alias name, date of birth, address, and social security number. Since the arresting officer does not know who he or she has just placed under arrest they use the name the suspect gives them. Some officers will attempt to verify the suspect's identity by fingerprinting them and running them through the system but this does not always happen and often when fingerprinting is completed no suspect information is returned. The suspect is booked under the victim's information and often given a small bond to make or even an OC bond,

Own Recognizance Bond or Signature Bond. The suspect is released from jail and given a date to return to court. Since the suspect did not use his or her real name and identifiers, they will not be returning to court to face the charges. When the court date arrives and the suspect does not appear, the Judge of the Court will issue a bench warrant for his or her arrest for FTA. Since the suspect used the victim's information, the FTA warrant is obtained and issued in that name. A few days or weeks later, an officer assigned to arrest the suspect on the outstanding warrants will locate the victim and arrest him or her and then transport them to jail. Sometimes, the victim may be driving down the road and, for what ever reason, is stopped by an officer. The officer may run a criminal wants or warrants check on the victim and discover that the victim has a failure to appear warrant. The officer will then arrest the victim for the FTA. Some agencies, before ever executing an arrest warrant, will verify the wanted person by a photograph of that wanted person compared with the person being detained but this does not always happen.

Some people believe that they are immune to such criminals, but these criminals are so efficient at obtaining information on someone that everyone is a potential victim. One of my first cases, after being promoted to detective, was a clever individual who could obtain all of the information needed to steal a person's identity within a couple of hours. This particular individual lived in a large apartment complex and several residents of the complex had filed identity theft reports. I probably would have never identified and apprehended the suspect, if not for his addiction to crystal methamphetamine. The suspect became careless and I was eventually able to identify him. After his arrest, we obtained a search warrant for his residence searching for evidence to his existing crimes and possibly evidence concerning numerous other crimes. I was amazed at the amount of information that this one suspect had collected and possessed inside of his apartment. We discovered boxes full of credit reports belonging to past, present, and future victims. I also discovered that this one suspect was able to obtain the credit reports of three very famous and prominent celebrities. It just goes to show that anyone can become a victim of identity fraud or identity theft at any time.

Many victims find that clearing their credit histories can be a very long and stressful ordeal. Victims of identity fraud have been delayed and sometimes disapproved for mortgages, vehicle loans, student loans, credit cards, and personal loans. Victims not only spend their time to clear such frauds but they also incur an enormous expense, as a whole, attempting to clear their good name. Victims will spend their hard earned money on telephone calls, stationary, stamps, and even legal fees to clear their names. Some victims even hire private detectives, in an attempt, to find out who stole their identity. Victims of identity fraud will lose wages because of the fraud and some even have their wages garnished by the creditor who received the fraudulent account. It is a crime that may continue to haunt the victim for years to come.

As I have mentioned, a person can not prevent identity fraud from happening. All that a person can do is attempt to limit the number of ways that their personal and financial information can be obtained and to keep a close watch on your information to limit the amount of frustration, stress, and money it may cost the person to repair the identity fraud.

If you do become a victim of identity fraud, file a police report either with your local jurisdiction or the jurisdiction where the actual fraud occurred. Since determining the exact location of an identity fraud can sometimes be very difficult and because most of the crimes committed by the identity fraud suspect are usually committed in a jurisdiction far away from the victim's location, several states have passed identity fraud statutes to allow for the victim to file a report with the jurisdiction where he or she lives. This has been done, in an effort, to assist the victim because numerous victims in the past have gotten the run around by jurisdictions not willing to assist the victims in their time of need. Filing a police report in Atlanta for an identity fraud that occurred in Los Angeles or vice versa will not necessarily result in an investigation conducted by the agency where the victim resides but can assist the victim in the identity fraud process required by many businesses.

I recommend that the victim of an identity fraud investigate as much as he or she can and obtain pertinent information. The victim also needs to file a report with every jurisdiction where a crime occurred. Identity fraud perpetrators will often commit several crimes in different jurisdictions and the possibility that the suspect or suspects can be identified and arrested will be increased. If, by chance, the victim does discover the suspect's or suspects' identities, they should never attempt to confront the suspect(s) and under no circumstance attempt to make an apprehension, this should be only completed by law enforcement personnel. Everyone must assume that all confrontations with individuals accused of any criminal act will become violent. Law enforcement personnel receive specialized training, weapons, and assistance, if needed, to apprehend and arrest such violent people which the average citizen does not possess.

In addition to filing police reports, the identity fraud victim needs to file a complaint with the Federal Trade Commission, send each business that the fraud suspect has obtained credit or made purchases a copy of a notarized fraud affidavit, return and answer any demand letters sent by a business, and keep a log of all of their activities such as who was contacted, when, and why. The victim needs to place a fraud alert on their credit history with a credit reporting agency. It is important to note that this initial fraud alert, verbal or through the internet, only lasts for 90 days. An extended alert is available that can last for a period of 7 years and can often be requested by the victim of an identity fraud if they write and send the credit reporting agency a letter requesting an extended alert accompanied by a police report. All three credit reporting agencies and several private businesses offer identity fraud monitoring for a fee and will notify the victim within 24 hours to 1 week of any major changes in their credit report. This helps but will not prevent identify fraud. It will help you to identify the fraud more quickly and may help cut your losses. At a minimum, monitor your credit report every six months. Most states require the three major credit reporting agencies to offer at least one free credit report per year to citizens of that state and in a few states, such as Georgia, the citizen can receive two free credit reports each year. Monitor your reports closely and have any incorrect information removed from the contents.

Chapter Six

Credit Card Fraud

Credit card fraud or financial transaction card fraud is the illegal and unauthorized use of a person's credit card, check card, or ATM card. In Georgia, simply possessing two or more credit cards issued to other people is prima facie evidence to arrest the suspect for financial transaction card theft. Financial transaction card theft differs from financial transaction card fraud in that theft means the mere possession and fraud means the actually use of the credit card or check card. Credit card fraud is one of the largest areas of crime that law enforcement investigates. It can also be an extremely difficult case to make. In Atlanta and throughout the nation, credit card fraud can often provide the fraud perpetrators with the means to facilitate other criminal acts such as drug use and drug sales. The Major Fraud Unit has investigated hundreds of these cases. These credit card fraud perpetrators can be organized, semi-organized, or independent.

The organized credit card fraud ring exists pretty much in the same manner as other organized criminal enterprises. Often the ring will deal in both credit cards and counterfeit checks. The mastermind of the organization will recruit individuals as their runners; these are referred to as his or her soldiers or mules. The mastermind or someone the mastermind trusts will then give the stolen credit cards or counterfeit credit cards to the runners who, in turn, use the credit cards to make purchases. After the runners have made purchases for merchandise, they give the merchandise to the mastermind or someone the mastermind has entrusted for this particular job. The merchandise is then fenced or resold in another area of the country or another country altogether.

The mastermind can collect stolen credit card information in a variety of ways. This suspect will often recruit individuals in banking institutions or other businesses that deal in a lot of credit cards. This individual is referred to as a mole. The mole will obtain the information for the main suspect and will be paid a fee for his or her services. The mole may be employed by a financial institution, medical institution, or any business that deals with a lot of credit card transactions.

The second method that the main suspect has is to recruit people working as waiters or waitresses. The main suspect will supply these individuals with a skimming device and they use this device to capture all of the information contained upon the magnetic strip of the victim's credit card. The skimmer will usually do this as they leave the table with your credit card. Efficient skimmers can go undetected for several months and rarely are caught in the act of skimming. The entire process takes just a few seconds. The server will remove the skimming device from his or her person, swipe your credit card through the skimming device, and then place the device back in their pocket or apron. The sale is processed and the server returns the credit card back to you. The skimming device is then hooked up to a personal computer or laptop and the stolen information is downloaded.

The main suspect might elect to place a skimming device on a banking institution's ATM or automated teller machine. These devices can be made to look like part of the machine. The fraud perpetrator will go to great lengths to fool their victims. In the past, this type of skimming device was bulky and did not look like part of the ATM. These machines were still able to fool some people and capture their credit card or check card information. More recent skimming devices on ATMs actually look like part of the machine. I can recall the first time that I responded to a call regarding this type of skimming device. I had to be shown where it was located because it looked like part of the ATM. These more current devices will be attached to the ATM over the card insert slot. These devices are small, battery operated, and the fraud perpetrator will usually attach them to the ATM by using two sided masking tape. The victim will feed their ATM card or credit card into the machine passing through the skimming device. As their card passes thru the device, the device captures the information on the card's magnetic strip. The victim will make his or her transaction and then receive their card back never knowing that the card had just been skimmed. This skimming method captures the information but does not capture the personal identification number or P.I.N. Some very clever fraud perpetrators have also found ways to steal this also. They have placed a fake keyboard over the machine's keyboard which will capture the P.I.N. as the victim presses the numbers. The perpetrator will then match the stolen account number with that of the stolen P.I.N.

In addition, to the aforementioned methods, fraud perpetrators can purchase stolen credit card numbers from other perpetrators or the fraud perpetrators can steal records and statements from businesses to obtain that information. Most experienced fraud perpetrators know exactly which businesses are easy targets and where these businesses keep and store records which contain personal and financial identifiers such as credit card numbers.

After the main suspect has obtained the credit card information, they can use this information on counterfeit credit cards. The more experienced fraud perpetrators will take the information which had been stolen, purchase blank credit cards, download the information to the magnetic strip, imprint the card with the account number and a name, and then counterfeit the card to appear as an original complete with a logo. After doing this, the fraud perpetrator's runners usually go to stores and make purchases for luxury items such as electronics, jewelry, perfume, or clothing. These items are then brought back to the main suspect who arranges for the merchandise to be fenced. Last year, in Atlanta, two suspects were arrested for financial transaction card fraud. The two suspects or mules were a female and a male who had flown in to Atlanta from New York with the sole purpose of committing fraud. The suspects, over a three day trip, purchased over $60,000 in merchandise using counterfeit cards complete with information on the magnetic strip. This fraud ring had taken the stolen account number of the credit card, removed the victim's name, and submitted an alias name of the suspect on the credit cards and magnetic strips. It is believed that these two mules alone were responsible for over $500,000 in fraudulent purchases to the Atlanta area within a few months. Once they purchased the merchandise with the counterfeit cards, they shipped the merchandise back to New York.

Shortly after these two suspects were arrested, another suspect was arrested attempting a similar credit card fraud. This particular ring of fraud perpetrators did not possess the ability to reproduce the information on the magnetic strip. However, the counterfeit cards were of excellent quality. The mule had flown to Atlanta with instructions to purchase luxury watches from area jewelry stores. The suspect would enter the stores, pick a particular watch, and then pay for the watch using one of the counterfeit credit cards. The employee of the store would attempt to swipe the card but since the magnetic strip was blank, received no response. The suspect would tell the employee that he worked in a hospital around x-ray machines and his credit card probably had been damaged. The employee would then key in the account number and receive approval for the sale. The suspect would then exit the business and give the watch to another suspect. This other suspect would then take the watch to the rented vehicle and place the watch inside of the vehicle. The mule would continue shopping until all of the jewelry stores had been hit or he was arrested. In this case, he was arrested. One employee of a jewelry store smelled a rat and contacted the police. The second suspect witnessed the arrest and immediately left the area with the stolen watches. This one shopping trip of counterfeit cards produced about $27,000 in stolen watches for the ring.

Most credit card fraud perpetrators do not possess the knowledge to fabricate counterfeit cards or know someone who can furnish them with counterfeit cards. This type of credit card fraud perpetrator will usually do one of four things to commit credit card fraud. These four are steal your credit card number and then use your number to purchase merchandise or services, steal your credit card and then use the stolen card, steal your identity and order a credit card in your name and then use the credit card, and by reinstating one of your closed accounts. All of the crimes are done without the victim's knowledge and may go undetected for several months.

One method which is very common is for the fraud perpetrator to obtain your credit card number and the three digit security number on the back. The fraud perpetrator can obtain this information in a variety of ways, they can copy the numbers down of a piece of paper after you make a purchase or perhaps paid a bill, they can copy the numbers by achieving access to the printed records that are produced after a purchase, steal the records from a business storage room or office, stealing confidential mail, and obtain the information through dumpster diving or rummaging through the garbage. Once the fraud perpetrator has obtained your credit card information in this way, they can use that information to purchase merchandise or services on your account.

I have investigated cases were the fraud perpetrator obtained someone's credit card information and then went online to made a purchase or even called the order in. The fraud perpetrator will then arrange for the item or merchandise to be shipped to a location such as a vacant building, residence, or an apartment. The suspect or someone connected to the perpetrator will then wait nearby for the package to arrive. Often, they will meet the delivery person and obtain the package directly from that person. The fraud perpetrator using this method of credit card fraud has entered businesses and purchased merchandise or services. When the fraud perpetrator goes to the cash register to pay for the merchandise, they tell the employee behind the register that they don't have their credit card on their person or perhaps lost their credit card. They tell the employee that they have the credit card number and ask the employee if the employee can look up their account in the system. Some stores have procedures for this type of sale and some require the customer to produce some sort of identification to complete the sale. More often than not, the fraud perpetrator is able to complete the sale and walk out of the business with the merchandise. The victim will discover the fraudulent transactions when he or she receives their monthly statement from the bank or credit card company. Sometimes, the victim does not look at their monthly statement and will go ahead and make the payment for the fraudulent charges. If this takes place, the crime goes undetected.

My wife and I were victims of fraud a few years ago. My wife called me, one day, advising me that something was wrong with her vehicle. She said that there was transmission fluid leaking out from underneath the vehicle and the car would not change gears. Since she was already in the parking lot of where she worked and I was on duty, I told her to call a local transmission shop and have them look at the car. She found one in the phone book and they came out and got the car. After towing the car back to the shop, an employee of the business called her informing her that she needed a new transmission and he could put one in for her for $2400. She called me with the news. Since the car was only three years old and had never given us any problem before, I suggested that she call the local transmission shop in our home town. They agreed to send a tow truck to the first shop and pick up the vehicle. When the tow truck arrived at the shop, my wife received a telephone call from the employee who told her that they could not release the vehicle until their tow bill had been paid. Since my wife worked across town from the shop and had no transportation to get over there, at that moment, she paid the tow bill by giving her ATM card number to the transmission shop's employee over the telephone. Later on that same day, the second shop called her and told her that she just had a plugged vent hose. The shop unstopped the clogged vent hose and added some new transmission fluid. The cost of their repairs and the tow bill was a little over $100 dollars. The vehicle ran like a new one after that. That afternoon, I drove to her workplace and brought her home.

A few days later, she went to the ATM to make a withdrawal. When she attempted the withdrawal, the transaction was denied. She checked the balance on our account and it revealed that we were overdrawn. She immediately went inside the banking institution to inquire about the balance. The bank's customer service representative retrieved the account in the system and told my wife that several purchases had been made at an electronic store in the same city that she worked. My wife told the customer service representative that she had not used her card at any such location. As she was completing the fraud and forgery affidavit, she called to tell me what had happened. I immediately left work, still in uniform, and met her at the bank. We then drove to the electronic store in the other city. As we arrived at the store, I requested assistance from the city's police department. An officer arrived and I explained the situation to him. We then went inside of the business and spoke to the owners about the fraudulent charge. When I asked about the charge, one of the gentlemen behind the counter said, in a very low voice, "Son of a bitch". This gentleman then proceeded to retrieve a receipt from underneath the counter. The officer with us then asked the owners who had made the fraudulent transaction and one of the owners said, "The employee at the transmission shop, he said that the card number was his grandmother's." The officer that was with us then requested a detective and he responded to the scene. The detective acquired statements and then obtained arrest warrants for the dishonest employee of the transmission repair shop. He was arrested for the crime shortly thereafter. It took us several weeks before all of the funds were replaced into her account. Needless to say, it was a lesson learned.

The second method of the fraud perpetrator is to actually steal your credit card. These fraud perpetrators can obtain your credit card by "creeping", pick pocket, purse snatching, burglaries, and entering vehicles. The creeper receives his or her name because of the way that they usually commit their criminal acts. The creeper will enter a business pretending that they belong in the location. He or she will usually try to pick a busy office with a lot of people. They will often dress to the occasion wearing business suits, dresses, slacks, or perhaps nice casual clothing. They will enter an office building and walk through the halls searching for offices. If they are stopped by an employee of the building, the creeper will often tell the employee that they are looking for a particular office or a particular employee that works in the building. All too often, the creepers are given the helpful directions and allowed to continue on their devious way. The creeper knows that people feel safe in their office or cubicle just like they would be if they were inside their own residence. The creeper knows that most women will enter their office or cubicle and place their purse containing their wallet either beside their desk or inside of an unlocked drawer and men will often hang their dress coat containing their wallet in the office or perhaps on the back of their chair. The creeper searches the building looking for offices or cubicles such as this and his or her only requirement is that the employee of the office be away from their desk or cubicle. Once the creeper locates such an area, he or she will quickly steal the wallet containing the victim's credit cards, information, and currency. This type of perpetrator is also known to steal laptops which have been left unattended.

I have worked a lot of cases involving creepers. Every so often, we had numerous creepers working the business district of Atlanta. One such case involved a well dressed individual. We began receiving numerous reports of thefts from buildings associated with several fraud reports. I was the responding officer on many of these reports and gained a first hand knowledge of what was occurring on my beat. After taking a police report from a lady regarding the theft of her credit cards from her wallet, she called to inform me that one of her credit cards had been used to make a purchase at a local store. I obtained as much information regarding the purchase as I could from the victim and then drove to the store's location. The store possessed digital video surveillance and had an excellent Asset Protection manager and team. Armed with the information, the Asset Protection team was able to capture the suspect on video surveillance. I asked if they could print me a still photograph of the suspect. The Asset Protection Manager not only printed one copy of the suspect but gave me about twenty five additional copies. I knew that the suspect had been working the area hard and immediately following his creeping adventures; he would go to a local department store and use the stolen credit cards. I took the surveillance photographs of the suspect and gave them to loss prevention managers throughout my beat and advised each of the suspect's M.O. or Modus Operandi.

A few days after obtaining the suspect's photograph, I received a telephone call from one of the store managers requesting that I come to the location. Upon my arrival, the loss prevention manager and his employees were smiling at me. As I inquired as to what was going on, the loss prevention manager pointed toward one of their holding cells. I opened the door and there was my suspect. The loss prevention manager told me that one his employees recognized the suspect from the photograph that I had given them and spotted the suspect as he entered the business. They watched the suspect attempt to purchase some clothing items using a stolen credit card. The loss prevention manager was able to contact the card holder before the completion of the transaction and confirm the card as stolen. As the suspect was attempting to exit the store, loss prevention employees detained him and took him to the loss prevention office. I advised the suspect of his Constitutional Rights and placed him under arrest. The suspect did not possess any form of identification and gave me a false name or alias which was not on file. I contacted Detective Cooper and he also responded to the scene. We then took the suspect to our Identification Section and had the individual fingerprinted. Our Identification Section could not return any information on the suspect but Detective Cooper was able to positively identify the suspect through another agency's Identification Section the following day. The suspect was charged accordingly and spent a couple of months in jail for his crimes.

After his release from jail, the suspect was placed on probation. About a year of so after his release, other jurisdictions began experiencing problems with a particular creeper. One detective obtained some video surveillance photographs of the suspect and emailed them to law enforcement agencies and security personnel asking if anyone could assist in identifying this suspect. Detective Cooper and I both recognized the suspect because it was the same individual we had dealt with earlier. The detective was contacted and given the information on his suspect. The detective obtained warrants for the suspect and shortly thereafter made the arrest.

Another case involved two employees of the same business. One of the employees was the victim and the other was the suspect. The employees of this particular business each were assigned a locker in the rear of the business to keep their personal belongings while they were working. The victim reported to work, placed her purse and wallet in her locker, clocked in, and went to work. When it came time for her first break, she went to her locker to remove some funds for a snack and discovered that someone had stolen her driver's license and credit cards. The victim immediately reported the incident to the store's asset protection or loss prevention manager. The manager notified me of the incident and I responded to the location. As I was driving to the location, the victim and the asset protection manager notified the victim's financial institution of the theft of the credit cards. One financial institution advised the victim that two charges had been made to her account that morning and both charges were at the location of the business. The asset protection manager obtained the information regarding the two fraudulent charges and was able to retrieve excellent video surveillance footage of the suspect. The asset protection manager immediately recognized the suspect as another employee of the business. Upon my arrival, the asset protection manager explained the situation. We then proceeded to interview the cashiers at each location where the suspect had committed the fraudulent transactions. Each of the cashiers positively identified the suspect as the person making the charge with the stolen credit card. I obtained the signed sales receipts for each transaction and the video surveillance photographs as evidence. The suspect was then arrested and charged with the crimes. After advising the suspect of her Constitutional Rights, the suspect stated that she did not know what all this was about. A search of the suspect, after the arrest, revealed the stolen credit cards and the driver's license of the victim.

Around the same time period, we also began receiving a lot of reports regarding thefts from health and fitness clubs. Atlanta, just like every other major city, has a lot of gyms, exercise, and fitness clubs. The reports all stated that a gym locker had been broken into and the victim's credit card and driver's license had been stolen. Some victims later filed addendums to the original report stating that the stolen credit card had been used at area merchants.

These locations contained shower rooms for both men and women and lockers where the customers can place their clothing and personal items. I went to several of the business locations and interviewed the managers. In each incident, there wasn't any video surveillance available because it is not allowed in areas such as bathrooms or locker rooms and there weren't any witnesses to any of the thefts. We dusted just about every locker that the perpetrator(s) had hit for latent fingerprints but all we were able to lift were partials or the victim's prints.

Our big break came when I received a telephone call from an administrator of a church located on Peachtree Road in the Buckhead area of Atlanta. I responded to the location and spoke with the church's administrator. She said that the church had a gym and workout area in the back and members had been complaining about numerous thefts from their lockers. We had not known about these incidents because, up to that time, the victims had just filed complaints with the church and not with the police department. The administrator said that the thefts had become such a problem that they had to install video surveillance cameras in the hallways leading to the locker rooms. She said that earlier that day, another member had reported another theft from his locker. We reviewed the video surveillance footage and watched as two suspects approached the locker room. The two suspects were both males, one was black and the other one was white. The white male suspect waited outside of the locker room and acted as the lookout as the black male entered the locker room. A few minutes later, the black male came out of the locker room and the two then left the premises. The church's administrator said that she did not recognize either of the two males and that they were not members.

About a week after this incident, I received another telephone call from the church's administrator. The administrator told me that the suspects had returned to the location and were now shooting basketball. I told her just to keep an eye on them and I would be responding to her location. I was about ten or fifteen minutes away from the location and asked tactical radio if there were any units close by that could assist me. One thing about police officers, when one officer calls for backup, they can usually count on someone responding. In this case, I had the assistance of three officers. I gave the lookout for the two suspects to the officers and made my way to the location. The three other officers were the first to arrive and immediately detained the two suspects.

Upon my arrival at the location, I began to interview the two suspects. The white male was the suspect of interest in the previous theft although I did not possess any concrete evidence that he had committed the crime. The black male suspect was not the suspect seen in the video surveillance of the previous incident but a new person of interest. I began to question the two and asked what they were doing at the location. The white male suspect told me in calm and cool manner that they were there to shoot some ball. I asked the suspect if they were members of the church and both responded "No, we are guests." I then asked them if they had used the lockers and the white male suspect said "yes" and pointed to a closed but unlocked locker. I asked if I could look inside and he said "Yeah, go ahead." I opened the locker and removed two gym bags and placed the bags on the bench. I asked if I could look inside of the bags and the white male suspect said "yes". As I opened the suspect's gym bag, I discovered some clothing, a lock still in the packaging, a small tool, and several small photographs of the suspect and a few unknown people. The white male suspect had been frisked for weapons as he was detained and the officer had discovered a large amount of currency inside of his pants pocket. I asked the suspect why he was carrying all that money and he replied that he had heard that someone had been breaking into the lockers and he was afraid that it might have been stolen. After discovering the new lock in the bag, I asked him why he had not locked the locker. The suspect told me that he had forgotten that he had the lock. As I continued the interview, I began to catch the suspect in lies. I contacted the Major Fraud Unit and a detective responded to my location. Prior to the detective's arrival, we separated the two suspects and placed them inside different patrol vehicles. At this time, the suspects were only being detained for questioning and we only suspected them of committing the thefts. The black male suspect was positioned inside of my patrol vehicle as we were waiting. The suspect was very nervous. He told me that he hadn't participated in any criminal activity but had been recruited by the white male to go to the location with him so that they could break into lockers.

After obtaining this information, we transported the two suspects to the Major Fraud office. The white male suspect would now be charged with criminal attempt to commit a crime. The two suspects were advised of their Constitutional Rights and each waived these Rights and made a statement. The white male made a statement and then I took him to another part of the office while the black male was making his statement. The white male who, at first, was calm and collected now began to become nervous. As we sat together, he began to ask me about his friend, the black male suspect. He then abruptly stated to me that his friend had committed no crimes and that today would have been the first time. The white male suspect then asked if I could help him out and I told him that he was the only one who could. The suspect then began telling me exactly how he had been committing the crimes and all of the people involved with the criminal activity.

The white male suspect said that he had also been recruited by another white male who lived in a very nice residence just west of Atlanta. The male suspect said that this white male ran a ring of fraud perpetrators which included about six other people. He stated that the crew was working fitness clubs and gyms from Tennessee, Georgia, Alabama, and Florida. He stated that they had discovered that, by the use of a small tool, a lock could be unlocked and entry gained to the locker. The suspect stated that after gaining entry into the locker, they would steal one credit card and the victim's driver's license. After stealing these two items, he said that they would lock the locker back. He added that if the lock had been damaged and would not lock back, they would replace the lock with a new lock. All of the victims of these crimes had complained that they had trouble opening their locks or that they had to obtain bolt cutters and have the lock cut off. The suspect stated that by stealing the two items and locking the locker back they were able to obtain the time necessary to complete any fraudulent purchases. The suspect told me that the reason for stealing the victim's driver's license was in case the store requested additional identification. Small passport photographs of the suspects were obtained prior to the thefts and would be installed over the picture of the victim. After doing this, the suspects would laminate the license.

The suspect described how he and the other suspects would then purchase electronic items such as laptops and work tools from various stores. After purchasing the items, they would take the items to the main suspect who paid them a small percentage of what the merchandise was actually worth. The main suspect would then fence the items through an online auction house doubling or even tripling his initial investment. I asked the suspect if he would be willing to cooperate with law enforcement to assist in the capture of the others and he responded that he would. I contacted the United States Secret Service Organized Fraud Taskforce and advised them of what we had. The U.S. Secret Service, through the suspect's cooperation, began to identify all of the suspects in the fraud ring. After several weeks of surveillance, the suspects were indicted by a Federal Grand Jury and arrested for their crimes. A search warrant executed at the main suspect's residence revealed numerous stolen tools and laptops still in their original packaging. Evidence was also collected that revealed the main suspect had been doing this for over ten years.

The pick-pocket perpetrator is a sneaky character just like the creeper and often operates in a manner that cannot be easily detected by the victim. The pick-pocket perpetrator can use several methods to obtain the goal, your wallet. Some will actually bump into you or have an accomplice bump into you while they steal your wallet from your pants pocket or purse. Some will wait for the opportune moment, such as a female leaving her purse inside of a shopping buggy as she shops. The pick-pocket will remove the victim's wallet as they are busy looking at the store's merchandise or grocery products. One of the most difficult set of cases that I worked was committed by several prostitutes or call girls. Most of these women were at one time or another, employed as prostitutes, strippers, or adult models. At times, these women made some pretty good money and at other times, not so good.

A couple of these girls, however, figured out a scheme that they could make several thousand of dollars a week and possibly even that amount in a day. The scheme was normally conducted by two suspects together but other cases involving just one suspect to as many as three suspects came across my desk. Normally though, two female suspects would cruise the bar area or nightclub district of Atlanta looking for a very intoxicated male to exit one of the bars. The victim was usually a person 25 to 40 years old and usually by himself. As the victim would be attempting to hail a taxi to return him to his hotel room, the two female suspects would drive up to him asking him if he wanted to party with them. The victim would think that he had just hit the jack pot. Here he is at 3:00 or 4:00 in the morning, all alone, and all night he had been trying to pick up someone. Now there are two women wanting to party with him. The victim would get inside of the vehicle and immediately one of the suspects would ask him for some gas money or some money to buy some beer. The suspects knew that most of these guys leaving the bar had spent most, if not all, of their currency inside of the bar. The victim, not wanting to disappoint his newly found girl friends would agree to pay for their gas or buy the beer. The female suspect driving the vehicle would then drive to the nearest ATM that had a drive thru. The victim would remove his ATM card from his wallet, insert it in the ATM, and then punch in his personal identification number or P.I.N. As the victim was doing this, the second suspect was "shoulder surfing" or obtaining the P.I.N. The victim removed the cash from the ATM, collected his card and receipt, and then placed the ATM card back into his wallet which was then placed back into his pants pockets.

The suspects and the victim would then leave the ATM and go to another location, which was usually a nearby parking area. The victim soon found both suspects making out with him. One of the female suspects would unbutton his pants and pull his pants down around his ankles. She would then commence giving the victim oral sex while, at the same time, removing his wallet. After removing his wallet, the suspect gave the wallet to the second suspect who, in turn, removed the ATM card from the victim's wallet. The first suspect still giving oral sex to the victim retrieved the wallet and replaced it back inside of the victim's pants pocket. When this was completed, the suspect stopped the oral sex and one of the two suspects immediately came up with a story that they needed to get home. The victim, now minus his ATM, would be dropped off at his hotel room or at a nearby convenience store that was still open. The two suspects would then proceed to the nearest ATM and begin making withdrawals, as many as possible, using the victim's P.I.N. Once this was completed, the suspects would then drive to an area 24 hour department store with self check registers and make purchases. The system would allow for the suspects to receive cash back up to a hundred dollars after each and every transaction. Usually, the suspects depleted the victim's bank account. If the account did not permit the suspects to receive any further cash, they would usually take the card to another department store and use the card as a credit card. We had an extremely large amount of reports regarding cases like these and the suspect information on most of them described different suspects.

At any given time, it was possible that several other women were working the same scheme. I was able to positively identify and arrest a few of the suspects. Two of the suspects who had perfected the scheme, almost ten years earlier, had combined arrests for prostitution and fraud. Because the crime was so successful, we felt that the information was being passed along to other women and some were even recruited so that she could be taught the crime by an experienced thief.

This type of case is difficult to solve. First, the victim is heavily intoxicated and his memory is affected. Second, the victims usually have a problem wanting to come forth and tell the truth- the exact truth about what happened. Some are married or have girl friends and are afraid that they will discover what they have done. Detectives are often left attempting to obtain the transaction details of the victim's ATM card from the victim's banking institution. After obtaining this, the detective will research all available transactions at various ATMs and retailers attempting to obtain any video surveillance footage of the suspect or suspects. If this is obtained, the next step is attempting to positively identify the suspect or suspects.

Every so often, law enforcement does get lucky in these cases. One, if we have knowledge of known suspects who use this M.O., we can possibly identify them through the use of quality video surveillance. The other method is to catch the suspects red handed and in the act. A few cases have lead to the arrests of several suspects when an officer or alert employee spots the suspects using the ATM card numerous times. In one such case, the officer noticed a vehicle with two females and a male at the ATM, early one morning, after the bars had closed. After making their transaction, the vehicle drove away from the ATM. Within about 30 minutes or so, the same vehicle was back at the ATM making a transaction or transactions. But this time, the vehicle was occupied by only two females. Because the veteran officer was experienced and he had knowledge of these types of perpetrators and their M.O., the officer had a reasonable articulable suspicion to make traffic stop on the vehicle and investigate. The officer's wise judgments lead to the arrest of these fraud perpetrators.

In another case, an employee of a 24 hour retail store noticed three female suspects passing an ATM card back and forth making purchase after purchase. The employee immediately notified 911 and carefully watched the suspects as they exited the store with the cash and merchandise. The employee was able to obtain the suspect's vehicle description and tag number as they exited the parking area. Shortly after, police arrived and the employee relayed the information to the officers. The officers placed a B.O.L.O. on the vehicle and another officer spotted the vehicle as the suspects were about to turn onto the onramp of the interstate. The officer made the traffic stop and after a brief investigation, all three suspects were arrested for credit card fraud.

An enormous amount of burglaries and larcenies from vehicles can be linked to the fraud perpetrator. Years ago, the criminal would break into your home, office, or car to steal something that they could sell or fence. In previous decades, a criminal would break into a vehicle to steal a car stereo. After obtaining the stereo, they would fence it for pennies on the dollar. In modern times, this criminal has discovered that by stealing a check book and/or credit cards, he or she can purchase as many as fifty of the same stereos. These criminals have discovered that a check book and/or credit cards can reward them far more greatly than a lot of other items or merchandise.

As was one such case I investigated in Atlanta. We had been receiving reports of someone breaking into vehicles throughout the zone. These reports would sometimes number as many as eight per day and had been going on for over two weeks in a row. It became such a problem that officers were placed on a detail to curtail the number of car break-ins and apprehend the perpetrator. The suspect would target different areas on different days and the only description of him which was given by two witnesses was a black male. Later, another witness to one of the incidents was able to give a description of the suspect's vehicle and obtained the tag number of that vehicle. The tag and the vehicle had been reported stolen from another jurisdiction earlier that month.

As that day started, so did the car break-ins. A veteran officer responded to the parking area of a local fitness club and took a report from a victim. The victim stated that she had left her purse inside of her vehicle while she went inside of the club and worked out. She discovered the incident upon finishing her workout and returning to her vehicle. The veteran officer asked what had been stolen and advised the victim to contact her financial institutions concerning the stolen credit cards and report any fraud occurring on the credit cards back to the police. Within one hour, the victim called the precinct advising that one of her credit cards had been used to make a $3,900 purchase at an electronic store. This information was forwarded to me since we had several of these stores in the area and on my beat.

I drove to an electronic store in close proximity to the location of the theft. Speaking with store's manager, I discovered that the store had just made a sale for $3900 which had been made by a white female driving a silver Mustang convertible. I inquired what the sale had been for and the store's management advised that she had purchased a flat screen television and two

DVD players. I asked if the store had delivered the merchandise and the store managers responded that they offered to but the lady had insisted on taking the merchandise herself. The managers told me that they had attempted to load the large flat screen television into the rear seat of the vehicle but it would not fit with the top down. Since it was beginning to rain, the female decided to call a taxi. The managers told me that the taxi arrived and they loaded the flat screen television in the rear seat. The suspect drove away with the taxi not far behind. I asked if she had presented any identification with the credit card and the managers told me that she had because of the store's policy. I asked if the name was the same on the credit card as that of the driver's license and they each replied "yes". I then asked if the picture on the driver's license was the same person who had made the purchase and again they replied "yes". I knew, at this point, that the suspect had taken the victim's identification and placed her picture over that of the victim and then laminated the license. It was the same information just a different picture and different person.

I contacted the officer who was working inside of the precinct that day and asked if he could assist me with the investigation. The officer began to call all the taxi cab companies in the area, asking each one if they had responded to the electronic store. The officer located the cab company and he notified me. Since we had officers assigned throughout the zone attempting to apprehend this suspect, I called the officer working the detail in that area and asked if he could swing by the cab company's location and speak with the cab driver that had responded to the electronic store. The officer went to the location and the owner of the cab company called the driver in. The cab driver told the officer that he had picked up the television and had followed the female suspect to an apartment building in Northeast Atlanta. After arriving at the complex, he helped her unload the television and take it inside one of the apartments.

The taxi driver could not remember the exact apartment but told the officer that he could show him the exact apartment. Since the officer was on a motorcycle, another officer responded to the cab company and transported the taxi driver in an unmarked patrol vehicle to the apartment complex. The taxi driver pointed to the silver Mustang parked in the parking area and then he pointed to the upstairs apartment stating that was the apartment he took the television to. We sat up a perimeter around the complex and I notified the Major Fraud office of what I had. The detective obtained a search warrant for the apartment and responded to our location. We executed the search warrant, recovered the stolen merchandise, and arrested four individuals. After securing all the suspects, another officer and I exited the apartment and walked down the stairs. As we entered the parking area, I noticed a vehicle matching that of the B.O.L.O. we were detailed for. The officer ran a check on the vehicle and it came back as reported stolen from the other jurisdiction.

Inside of this vehicle was evidence of perhaps 50 car break-ins and inside of the suspect's apartment, we discovered the key to the vehicle. After this, the reports of car break-ins greatly reduced. No doubt, we had captured the person responsible. This person was the main suspect in a small fraudulent ring committing larcenies from vehicles. This ring's sole purpose was to obtain credit cards and driver's licenses of victims so that they could make fraudulent purchases for merchandise which could be fenced.

Another method that a credit card fraud perpetrator will use can be obtaining a valid credit card in your name. This method requires the fraud perpetrator to obtain all of the necessary personal and possible financial information about you. In effect, the fraud perpetrator will steal your identity and pretend to be you. The fraud perpetrator can do this by stealing your mail and then complete a credit card application. The fraud perpetrator will then watch for the mail to be delivered and when the credit card arrives will steal it from your mailbox. The suspect will then activate the card and has a full month to use the credit card before anyone discovers the incident. The fraud perpetrator, if they have stolen your identity, will also complete a credit card application either through the mail or online using your personal identifiers. This type of credit card fraud perpetrator will have the card shipped to another address. This address usually is the same type of address where merchandise is shipped to, a vacant building, apartment, or residence. The fraud perpetrator or one of his or her associates will wait and watch for the card to be delivered. After receiving the credit card, the fraud perpetrator will again activate the card and proceed to purchase merchandise and services.

Another way is for the fraud perpetrator to obtain a copy of your credit report. The fraud perpetrator will look for accounts that have been closed by the consumer. Using your information, the fraud perpetrator will contact the bank or business regarding the closed account and request that the account be reinstated. The fraud perpetrator will then advise the bank or business that you have moved and give the bank or business an address to have the reinstated credit card delivered to. Again, the same type of address is given to the bank or business. If the fraud perpetrators are successful in obtaining credit cards in your name, you might not discover the fraudulent activity for one month or perhaps even several months after the crimes.

You can deter a lot of credit card fraud from occurring by simply being careful as to where you use the card. Because so many restaurants have hired people who have skimmed credit cards or are now currently skimming cards, some restaurants are changing the way people pay when using a credit card. The server, in these restaurants, will bring a portable device to your table. The server then will place the amount of the check into the machine, and then give the machine to the card holder. The card holder then swipes his or her credit card, check card, or ATM card through the machine. The machine will then deliver a receipt for the card holder to sign. The theory behind this system is if the card never leaves the hand of the card holder, the server cannot skim the card. No doubt, this will prevent a lot of skimming from ever occurring. But do not be fooled, the fraud perpetrator is often very smart and clever. He or she eventually finds a way to defeat the process. If you are using an ATM be especially mindful that fraud suspects will place skimming devices directly on the machine especially around the card insert slot. If this looks abnormal or if you can remove something from the machine, do not use the machine and contact your local police agency immediately and notify the banking institution. You might also want to think about reducing the number of credit cards and ATM cards that you carry inside of your wallet or purse. If they are stolen or lost, you could spend a lot of time trying to research and contact each banking institution or business. I would advise carrying one but no more than two such cards inside of your wallet or purse. Keep the others safely stored away in a safe or safe deposit box. Also, keep your cards safe while at work or at play. Keep your wallet on your person while at work. For women, I would recommend a fanny pack or something similar. Never place your wallet inside of any locker thinking that it is safe. Criminals will break the lock and make off with your valuables. Keep the wallet and its contents on your person. Never, ever, leave your wallet or purse in your vehicle in plain view. If it is not possible to take your wallet or purse with you, place it inside of the trunk area. Be especially mindful of anyone watching you do this because they can defeat this to. A suspect can break into a vehicle and then simply hit the trunk unlock device equipped on most vehicles. If you have all of the credit cards that you need, and most people have way more than they need, contact one of the three major credit reporting agencies and be placed on a do not send or do not contact list. This way, you can stop receiving credit card offers that come in through the U.S. mail. Last, but not least, pay special attention to your monthly bill.

Chapter Seven

Counterfeit Checks and Counterfeit Check Rings

One thing that the 21st Century has brought to the world of crime is the organized or semi organized fraud rings. These rings operate in just about every major city and it seemed as Atlanta was a major place for these criminals to set up shop. Law enforcement agencies will investigate counterfeit check fraud committed by an independent suspect and those crimes committed by the more advanced semi organized fraud rings or organized fraud rings. The main choice of weapons for today's check fraud perpetrator is a personal computer or laptop equipped with a quality printer.

This century has brought about many changes in the way we all conduct our daily business. Just about every business uses a computer or a system of computers to do their business. You can find personal computers or laptops in the majority of homes across America. The computer has inevitably become a major part of our everyday life. The fraud perpetrators have, as usually, taken something good and used that to their advantage. Armed with a computer or laptop and a good printer, the check fraud perpetrator has been able to steal an enormous amount of money from victims and businesses.

In the past, independent check fraud perpetrators usually consisted of three types of criminals. One type was the guy who stole a check which was an intended payment to someone else. After obtaining the stolen check, the check fraud perpetrator would then "wash" the check using ordinary household chemicals. By washing the check, he or she would remove most of the ink on the check paper which contained the pay to the order of information and often the amount of the check itself. This check fraud perpetrator would leave the signature of the account holder. This was done in case any signature comparisons were completed by the banking institution. After washing the check, the fraud perpetrator would then take the check to a banking institution and cash the check. These cases still exist in today's world but have become less common since the invention of the computer and high tech printers. This perpetrator will usually obtain their checks through the mail, stealing a check which was intended by the victim for a payment of some type.

The second type of check fraud perpetrator is the person that steals actual checks from citizens and businesses. These perpetrators have been known to "creep" inside of businesses, obtain checks through burglaries or by breaking into a vehicle. "Creepers" can usually be described as those committing a theft from the business while the business is open. The creeper will maneuver his or her way into the business and then steal business checks from the office. The creeper has also been known to steal personal checks, credit cards, laptop computers, and cash from the employees of the business. Once this type of check fraud perpetrator obtains the checks, he or she will then make the check payable to themselves or to an alias. If the fraud perpetrator does the latter though, they must obtain a counterfeit identification card which will pass the scrutiny of any bank teller. These crimes also exist in today's time but are becoming less in numbers.

Office creepers who steal checks will enter the business during working hours. These criminals will usually target smaller businesses that have only one or two employees working in the office. These check creepers will wait for the employee or employees to become distracted and then go through the office desks until they find the business' checkbook or even a checkbook belonging to one of the employees. The creeper is very sneaky by nature and, usually, will not steal the whole book of checks. If the creeper does this, the theft will be noticed quicker and the owner will have the account closed. The check creeper will remove three to six checks from the rear of the checkbook and then exit the business undetected. Since the theft of the checks is not discovered immediately, the check fraud creeper now has time to cash these checks. The check fraud creeper may attempt to cash the checks themselves using their own name or perhaps an alias using a counterfeit identification card. The check creeper will also recruit "runners" to cash the checks for them. These individuals will receive a portion of the funds for their services which is usually 10 to 25 percent of the amount of the check.

I worked a high profile case involving a professional sports athlete who had been victimized by an individual he and his wife had befriended. The victims had met this character at a local car wash and decided to hire the suspect to help out around the house with odd jobs. The couple paid the suspect generously for his time whenever he worked for them. Within a short period of time though, the suspect began to steal from the couple. The suspect was able to gain access to three of the couple's accounts at three different financial institutions by stealing their checkbooks which he found in their vehicles and home. After stealing these checks, the suspect began to write his own ticket so to speak. At first, the suspect began to write and cash these checks in amounts that he would normally receive for his labor from the couple. After writing several checks, he soon realized that he was getting away with it. He then began to write checks, pretty much on a daily basis, for thousands of dollars. The suspect was able to do this for several months before the stolen money was noticed.

Professional athletes, actors, and musicians are often targeted because of their earnings. Many have accountants and financial advisors that keep track of their finances. The couple became aware of the theft, which was in excess of $100,000, and confronted the suspect. The suspect denied the allegations and broke off all contact with the victims. The victims filed a police report and after an extensive investigation, I obtained arrest warrants for the suspect for the forgeries and thefts. The suspect went on the run and it took our fugitive unit several months to locate and capture him for the forgeries.

The third type of check fraud perpetrator was more of an artist. This fraud perpetrator usually made his checks or had knowledge of printing to make his or her checks appear authentic. These perpetrators were rare. A good fraud perpetrator equipped with counterfeit checks of excellent quality usually had the knowledge of how to pass them. Some of these perpetrators were able to steal more than a million dollars in their lifetime. These fraud perpetrators paved the road for the check fraud perpetrators of today.

The check fraud perpetrator of today does not have to rely on his or her artistic ability or have to have the ability to run a printing press. The check fraud perpetrator of today just needs the ability to operate a personal computer or a laptop equipped with a quality printer. Just about everything he or she needs can be easily obtained from any office supply store, department store, or ordered through the World Wide Web. Anyone can purchase check stock, ink, and the program to print your own checks. This will cost the check fraud perpetrator anywhere between $25.00 and $50.00. All he or she now needs is the information to imprint on the counterfeit checks and they are in business. Many fraud perpetrators will take the next step in the criminal endeavor and either fabricates or purchases a fake identification card to allow them to complete transactions.

About eight years ago, I came across a check fraud perpetrator from Florida who would come to Atlanta with the specific intentions of making fraudulent transactions. The suspect would search the classifieds of the paper to locate people who were selling expensive jewelry especially those that were selling diamond rings. Most of the victims were selling a family heirloom which they had inherited. The suspect would contact the victim via the telephone, give them a false name or alias, and ask all of the right questions concerning the ring. Of course, the suspect wanted to see the ring before he ever bought it so he would set up a meeting with the victims.

The key to this scam, however, was the day and time of the meeting. The suspect always arranged for the meeting to take place on a Saturday afternoon and in a public place. He would meet with the victim and the victim would show him the ring. After a few minutes, the suspect would tell the victim he would purchase the ring. The suspect then gave the victim a cashier's check which had already been made out for the victim's selling price. The suspect would leave the restaurant with the diamond ring and the victim would leave with the check. Since it was Saturday, the victim had to wait until Monday morning to cash the check or deposit it into his or her account. On Monday, the sellers discovered that the cashier's check was counterfeit and that they were now victims. The suspect had given the victims a fake name and address. The telephone number he used came back to a prepaid cellular telephone company which did not require the suspect to give any personal information to have the phone activated. We were able to identify the suspect, however, through one victim. This victim had become suspicious of the suspect and after the transaction had been completed, followed the suspect to his vehicle. The victim was able to obtain the Florida tag number on the suspect's vehicle.

Victims, of this type of fraud perpetrator, do not realize that the check is counterfeit until several days after the transaction. Between the time of the transaction and the victim discovering that the check was counterfeit, the fraud perpetrator is long gone. The safest way to complete any transaction involving cashier's checks, money orders, and personal checks are for the victims not make the sale until they are able to verify that the cashier's check, personal check, or money order is valid in all shape and form. This will include the amount of the check. Fraud suspects have been known to obtain a valid cashier's check or money order in a lesser amount and then counterfeit the original check or money order to reflect an amount which is greatly increased. If you are thinking of conducting any such transaction, I would recommend that you do so during the time that banking institutions are open and you can verify the payment before ever selling your item.

One trait of check fraud perpetrators that is becoming more and more common is the fact that they are taking less risk. A lot of check fraud perpetrators will acquire the information needed to imprint the checks either by stealing the information or having someone else steal the information for them. Some check fraud perpetrators after procuring this information and counterfeiting checks will locate someone to run the checks for them. The runner or mule will receive a percentage of the checks while, at the same time, take all of the risks. This type of system has allowed for a more clever check fraud perpetrator who is now able to avoid being discovered by law enforcement and has led to a more advanced scheme, the check fraud ring.

The organized check fraud ring can be as small as three or four people or it can be as large as twenty or more people. Many check fraud rings operate with one or two individuals at the top. These perpetrators will often refer to their operation as a "house". We have discovered several "houses" operating and existing side by side. The top people of the check fraud ring will recruit and train several middle men or women to help them facilitate their illegal and counterfeit checks. These middle men or women are taught to recruit other people as runners or mules. Usually within any ring, the mules are the first to be arrested. Only after several arrests of different mules with the same type of counterfeit check does an agency realize that a ring is operating in the area. Mules often do not possess a great deal of information about the ring and when debriefed will often lie to the detective in an attempt to reduce the charges or perhaps the amount of jail time. The mules are quite often homeless people or people down on their luck. The middle man or woman searches the area for people such as this because they know that most of the individuals are willing to take the chance. Mules that are recruited by these middle men must possess a valid identification card or driver's license and social security card so that they can pass the counterfeit check.

There are various methods to this general scheme and all have been successful to different extremes. One method used by these fraud rings is to obtain the checking account information from a victim's account. This can be either a personal checking account or a business account. When the mastermind obtains this information, they will have their middle men or women take to the streets for the purpose of recruiting the runners or mules. Once the middle man or woman locates several of such people to be their runners, the middle man or woman will obtain their information from their identification cards or driver's license. The middle man will then inform the runners to meet him back at the location the following day at a specific time. The middle man will then pass the runner's information on to the mastermind. The mastermind will then fabricate counterfeit checks using the personal information of the mules or runners combined with the stolen account information.

Sometimes these counterfeit checks are personal checks and, at times, business checks. After the checks have been made, the middle person will take the checks and pick up the runner at the designated place and time. The middle person will then provide transportation to and from the banking institution or business for the runner. As the runner enters the banking institution or business, the middle person keeps a watchful eye on him or her. One, they do not want the runner to run away with their money after cashing the check and most importantly, want to know if the runner is discovered and the police are responding. If the runner decides to keep the money and go out the back door, it's a good bet the middle person will track them down with the intentions to hurt them or perhaps kill them. If the runner faces an arrest, the middle person will exit the area immediately upon police arrival. The middle person will then notify the mastermind that the runner has just been busted. One thing that makes these rings so difficult to investigate is that the runner cannot be used in any future setups conducted by the police to capture the middle person. Most check fraud rings will use a runner or mule until he or she is caught in the act. When this occurs, they will usually drop them completely breaking off all contact with the runner. Law enforcement has been successful in several cases using runners who have been apprehended when their arrests had not come to the attention of either the middle persons or the masterminds.

Check fraud rings are also known to use their counterfeit expertise to purchase merchandise. These fraud perpetrators will usually give the runner a shopping list which contains either electronic items or clothing items. The runner will enter a business armed with counterfeit checks and a fake identification card and then purchase the items on the shopping list. The runner will then exit the store with the merchandise and give the merchandise to the middle person. The following day, the runner or another person will attempt to return the items to the store for a refund. A lot of stores and retail businesses have systems which prevent returns such as these before the check is allowed to clear. There are still some stores that exist that do not have this measure. The fraud perpetrators know which stores that do and which stores that do not. If the fraud perpetrators can not return the items, they will often attempt to resell the items or pawn the items for a fraction of the item's cost.

One such counterfeit check fraud ring had been established by a very knowledgeable counterfeiter. This guy had an elaborate system set up and it took law enforcement several years to eventually gain enough evidence on this individual before he and his operation could be shut down. The Governor's Office of Consumer Affairs and the United States Secret Service Organized Fraud Task Force worked many long days on this ring obtaining the evidence to send this perpetrator and several of his co-conspirators to jail for a long time. The mastermind of the ring had different people inside of the crew which he referred to as his lieutenants and others he referred to as soldiers. The mastermind of the ring very rarely was around anything that would get him arrested but all of the money would lead directly back to him. He would then remove a percentage and pay all those that were involved in the criminal conspiracy.

This fraud perpetrator had employed different individuals to obtain stolen information, different people to receive the information, different people to obtain the fake documents and identification cards, different people for the middle men, and a lot of different people as runners. It was quite well organized. This particular suspect had people working secretively for him that worked in banks, hospitals, and health care centers. These individuals would obtain the stolen information and then receive funds for that information. The Governor's Office of Consumer Affairs conducted a forensic search of one laptop of this ring after they had been arrested. This one laptop contained the stolen personal information and counterfeit identification cards of over 2400 people. These suspects were very good at this type of criminal activity. They arranged for someone to steal the identities for them, made their own counterfeit checks and fake identification cards, and then knew exactly which banks and stores were the most susceptible to check fraud. An extremely large amount of counterfeit activity in Atlanta and the surrounding areas can be directly related to this crew.

Several years back, a check fraud ring busting counterfeit checks led to the homicide of a two year old child. The check fraud ring had been working Atlanta and its surrounding jurisdictions. The ring consisted of a pair of brothers who were the mastermind behind the criminal scheme. Both of the brothers had prior felony convictions but were currently out of jail. The two had recruited several people as middle persons and had numerous runners they used quite often. Law enforcement had begun to receive reports on several of the counterfeit checks but, for the most part, the ring had gone undetected. Then a tragic thing occurred just south of Atlanta. All of the news channels aired the story and it definitely was heart breaking. The news channels all reported that an apparent home invasion left a two year old child dead from gunshot wounds. The family told reporters and the police department that they had just came home from cashing their income tax refund check and that an unknown person broke into their home yielding a hand gun demanding the money. The father of the child said that he grabbed his weapon and a fire fight ensued inside of the residence. A bullet struck the little child, killing him. The story ran for several weeks and the hearts of people went out to the family of this small child. It was a very sad event.

A few weeks after the death of the small child, I received a telephone call from another detective who was working the Buckhead area of Atlanta. The detective told me that she had just received a call from a lady regarding some counterfeit checks which had been posted to her account. At that particular time, the Major Fraud Unit handled or at least was assigned all of the fraud related cases in Atlanta. The detective requested that I give this lady a call and I did. The lady stated that she needed to show me something and asked if I could come out to her residence. Upon my arrival at the location, I met with the lady concerning her checking account. The lady retrieved copies of five counterfeit checks which had been posted to her account. The checks were in the form of payroll checks and had names of people imprinted on the pay to the order line. The checks had all been made payable for less that $500 dollars each and the lady discovered the fraud when she discovered her checking account was overdrawn. Although the checks were not personal checks and did not contain her name and/or address, they went through her account because her account number was imprinted on the checks. I began to ask her how she thought her checking account had been compromised, she said that she thought a check she had mailed to a charity had been stolen because the check had not cleared and she had mailed it almost a month earlier. I asked if she had placed this check in her mailbox and she responded "yes". I thought to myself that the check was probably stolen from her mailbox and the suspects were definitely local. The lady then brought to my attention something that might have been overlooked by most other people. She had a copy of the paper from a few weeks earlier which the lead story was the funeral of the two year old child killed during the home invasion. In the article, the newspaper had a quote from the grandmother of the child. The lady then pointed to the copy of the counterfeit check and said, "Do you think there is a connection?" The name of the payee on the counterfeit check and the name of the deceased child's grandmother were the same. I gathered the copies of the five counterfeit checks and returned to the fraud office to begin my investigation.

Two of the five checks had been written to a female, two of the checks written to a male, and the fifth check to a different female. As I investigated the five counterfeit checks, I made a startling discovery. Two of the counterfeit checks had the name of the deceased child's grandmother as the payee, one of the counterfeit checks had the name of a very close friend of the family, and the other two counterfeit checks had the name of the child's father listed as the payee. I contacted the lead homicide investigator assigned to the case. I advised him of what I had discovered and that I would assist his investigation all that I could. The lead homicide detective on the case is an excellent detective and had discovered that the family of the deceased child was involved in a counterfeit check fraud ring and operated as runners for the ring. The investigation had discovered that the mother of the deceased child had just passed a counterfeit check and had not taken the funds to the middle person. The middle person, thinking that the mother had ripped them off, sent a person to collect the funds. When that person busted in the residence, the father grabbed his weapon and a fire fight commenced. During the fire fight, the small child was shot and killed. The suspect who had broken into the apartment fled the scene. Through excellent investigative and interview techniques, the homicide detective was able to identify and arrest the person who had shot and killed the two year old child and the middle person who had hired the hit man.

My investigation took me to several stores in several jurisdictions where the family had busted the counterfeit checks. None of the stores contained any type of video surveillance equipment but I was able to recover the original counterfeit checks from the store's loss prevention office. Although the stores did not possess any working video surveillance, they did require all of the people cashing checks, at any of their locations, to provide an inked fingerprint on the checks. The stores also required that the person cashing the check provide an identification card or driver's license which was recorded by the cashier on the face of the check. In these incidents, the suspects used their own identification cards. If questioned or apprehended at a later date, the suspects will try to convince law enforcement that they are a victim of identity fraud and someone else, not them, had cashed the check. To overcome this, I took all of the checks which had the inked fingerprints on the face to Identification Sections of various police departments. All of the suspects had a prior criminal history and their fingerprint cards were on file. Identification experts confirmed that the suspect's fingerprints were those on the checks. I obtained arrest warrants for identity fraud and forgery warrants for the father, aunt, and grandmother. A small child was dead because the family was committing crimes and to add to the situation, had lied to the general public who had opened up their hearts and pocketbooks to assist. I wonder if all those criminally involved in this case ever think about what they have done.

The two brothers who had masterminded the whole counterfeiting scheme did not have anything to do with the hit man. After the shooting incident, the two went on the run. One brother was arrested in Alabama. We had an enormous amount of evidence on him. We highly suspected the other brother was deeply involved in the scheme however we had no tangible evidence. He is still at large. The operation was shut down, at least temporarily.

The semi organized check fraud ring will obtain information similar to that of an organized check fraud ring. The major difference between the two is that the organized ring will have a tiered structure and the semi organized ring will not. The semi organized ring will not have a mastermind, so to speak, at the top of the ladder but will have several individuals within the group who are knowledgeable about fraudulent crimes. This type of organization will not usually recruit runners to pass the counterfeit checks but will teach a friend or an acquaintance how to obtain the information, make the counterfeit checks, and how to pass the counterfeit checks. The profit derived from the criminal incidents may be shared with several people within the ring but will not be split as a percentage among different individuals as the organized ring. Members of the semi organized rings will, at times, sell personal and financial identifiers of victims to friends or acquaintances for money, drugs, electronics, and even sex.

You can prevent a lot of check fraud or at least deter it. Limit the number of checks you write or, if possible, eliminate them all together. Check fraud perpetrators do not necessarily have to physically steal your checks to be successful. They can photocopy your personal check or they can just write the information down on a piece of paper. In today's world, all the fraud perpetrator needs is your information the rest is quite easy.

Check fraud in itself is a form of identity fraud. Whenever someone steals you're checking information and compromises your account, they are stealing your name, address, account information, and sometimes your telephone or driver's license numbers. Say, for example, that you go in to a store and make a purchase. You pay for the purchase by means of a personal check. On the check, the cashier writes your driver's license number and expiration date. You then exit the store with your newly purchased items on your way home. The cashier, after you leave the store, then reopens the register and removes your check from the register. The cashier then copies your information down on a piece of paper. The cashier obtains your name, address, telephone number, and driver's license number, the expiration date of your driver's license, routing number, and account number. After doing all of this, the cashier sticks the paper in his pocket or in her pocketbook. After they get off of work, they go home. When they arrive home, they proceed to use your personal information to produce books of checks on their personal computer or laptop and printer. The cashier or one of the cashier's close friends will then obtain a quality counterfeit identification card or counterfeit driver's license with your information on it. This may cost them as little as $25 or it may cost them $200. After obtaining the fake identification document, they are ready to make your life a living hell for some time to come.

I have investigated numerous cases were these suspects pass these counterfeit personal checks using your information at stores throughout town, stores in other cities, and even stores in other states. In some of these cases, the fraud suspect(s) were able to cash 20 or more counterfeit checks before finally moving on to another victim. The victim will first notice these counterfeit checks when he or she is either checking their account balance or their banking institution notifies them that a check or several checks has been returned because of insufficient funds.

You may have only a few checks clear your account before you discover the incident. You immediately notify your banking institution and fill out forgery and fraud affidavits. Your banking institution will close your account, issue you another account, and begin the process of refunding you what money had been stolen from your account which could take as long as two weeks. You are now pissed off but just when you think that you have it all back under control, something else occurs. When you discovered the counterfeit checks, you contacted your banking institution and they closed your account. Now, if the fraud perpetrator has written 20 such counterfeit checks and only three of those had cleared your account, what happened to the other 17? Since your banking institution has closed your account, they will not accept any checks written on that particular account from the time the account was closed. Therefore, your banking institution will send the checks back to the businesses where the suspects cashed them. The business will then send you demand letters, demanding payment plus a service charge for the check. You must now send each and every business an affidavit of forgery and even then you might not be able to convince the business that is was not you that had written the check. It is important to note that the victim should never ignore a demand letter in these situations. Unless you notify the business that the check is counterfeit, they will assume that it was returned from a closed account or perhaps for non sufficient funds.

Several states, including Georgia, view bad checks as a civil matter. By law, the business must present a demand letter to the victim requesting payment for the check and the business can impose a fee for this process. In Georgia, after ten days from the time you receive the demand letter and you have not paid the check amount and applicable fees, the civil matter can become a criminal matter. The business can do one of two things, they can apply for an arrest warrant, or they can turn the case over to the local law enforcement agency. Either way, you could face an arrest for a crime that you did not commit.

A lot of people pay their bills, purchase food, and clothing using their personal checks. Some people are still placing checks inside of an envelope and placing the envelopes in their mailboxes. I would recommend to all those who are still doing any of the aforementioned things to limit the number of checks they write and how they send their payments. Most banking institutions offer some type of program on their web sites so that people can pay their bills online. These sites are, for the most part secure and, safe to use. You can set up an account in a matter of minutes, designate when and how much you want to pay on each account, and keep a record of all payments. Whenever you schedule such a payment, your banking institution will deduct the funds directly from your account and then wire the funds to the intended recipient. The recipient will receive your funds in one or two business days. The most important factors of this type of method are that the recipient will receive a reference number which will reference your account. The recipient does not receive any of your checking account information as they would if you had written them a personal check. Plus, you won't have to worry about stamps and envelopes.

When shopping or purchasing merchandise, I would recommend that you pay using currency or a credit card and then immediately send a payment for the amount to the credit card company using your banking institution's web site and bill pay. Several people use their check cards to make purchases; this too, is relatively safe unless you are victimized by a skimmer. If your check card is compromised, it will be your funds that the perpetrators receive. Many banks will repay you part, if not all, of your stolen funds but this may take some time. If you have to send a payment to someone but cannot use your online bill paying method, credit card, or check card, I would recommend sending a cashier's check or perhaps a money order. That way, if it is stolen, the fraud perpetrators will not have access to your checking information. For all of the people that freely give their banking information to someone over the telephone or through the World Wide Web, remember that the security of your checking account information, as well as your personal information, is based entirely upon the honesty of the person or persons receiving that information.

Anyone can become a victim of a perpetrator when shopping or paying bills regardless of what payment method a person might use. If the victim's credit card or credit card number is stolen and used by a suspect, the victim will usually complete fraud affidavits with the particular financial institution that issued the credit account. If the victim's checking account has been compromised, the victim will discover that he or she will be completing fraud and forgery affidavits with their financial institution as well as other stores and businesses which had received the fraudulent instruments. I like to think that it is easier to address one problem than to have to deal with the same problem magnified many times over.

Chapter Eight

Counterfeit Currency

At any one time, there are millions of dollars in counterfeit currency in existence and being circulated throughout the United States. It is a huge problem and mainly investigated by federal authorities such as the United States Secret Service. Counterfeiting weakens the economy and jeopardizes the national security of this nation. People are always trying to cheat the system and counterfeiters are always trying to print "free money". Ever since the invention of currency, there are those that have attempted to copy it. This is why the United States Government uses security measures and procedures in our currency. Ever so often, the security features are changed or additional features added. This is all done to prevent counterfeiters from duplicating the currency and destroying our economy.

Counterfeiters of currency have used everything from printing presses to copiers. Some have even taken parts of different denominations of currency and placed them on lesser denominations of currency and have successfully passed them as the authentic currency. I have observed counterfeit currency which has been so bad that it was hard to imagine anyone, at all, accepting these bogus bills but some did. I have also seen counterfeit currency that was very difficult to distinguish from an authentic bill. The quality of the counterfeit currency will often depict the counterfeiter's success.

Jurisdictions will receive a lot of reports of counterfeit currency. Most of these reports are from businesses that have been victimized and have discovered the counterfeit currency during a tally of the daily receipts. An officer or detective will respond to the location, take the report, and seize the counterfeit bill or bills as evidence. The business is at a loss in the amount of the counterfeit bills. If a counterfeit bill goes undetected and is allowed to circulate into the economy, an individual might receive one or several counterfeit bills as change whenever they make a purchase. A person may not know that the counterfeit bill was not authentic and proceed to use the counterfeit bill or bills to make a future purchase or payment. This presents a huge problem for the innocent individual. To possess a counterfeit bill is a crime and to actual utter or pass the counterfeit note is another crime. Sometimes, a person will present a counterfeit note unknowingly and the business will alert law enforcement. The individual is detained, questioned, and may run the risk of being arrested for forgery. The responding officer or detective will usually use his or her discretion to make that decision. Either way, a police report is made and the counterfeit note or notes are seized as evidence. The individual is not given authentic currency to cover his or her loss. They are out the amount of the counterfeit note.

Criminal acts must have an element of intent. If the individual knows, or as a reasonable person should have known, that the note was counterfeit and attempts to or successfully pass the note or notes, then they can be arrested for the crime of forgery. I have made a few arrests involving people attempting to pass a counterfeit check. These arrests were made after I made the decision that the suspect knew the note was counterfeit and that they were attempting to deceive the business.

Most counterfeit notes are detected by financial institutions and businesses. However, some counterfeit notes do find their way into circulation. Whenever you receive change for something, be certain to look at the currency you receive. A person can often distinguish between an authentic note and a counterfeit note by the texture, color, and security measures. If, by chance, you are given a counterfeit note contact the manager immediately and alert law enforcement. The business, at its discretion, may refund you the amount of the counterfeit bill. Either way, law enforcement needs to respond, make a report, and seize the counterfeit bill as evidence. If you are uncertain about the authenticity of a note, you may take the note to just about any financial institution and they can advise you.

Chapter Nine

ATM Thefts

Fraud detectives will investigate a lot of criminal activities which occur around ATMs or automated teller machines. Sometimes, the criminal acts may be related to another criminal incident such as a pick pocket using the victim's debit card or credit card which had been stolen elsewhere or perhaps, it is the actual location of the crime. Either way, detectives usually find themselves at the location attempting to retrieve any physical or circumstantial evidence.

We had several ATM cases some years back and the same suspect was arrested several times. The suspect became quite well known in the law enforcement community and some officers even nicknamed him Candy Man. In the beginning, the suspect was approximately fourteen years old. He would obtain a carton which contained candy of some type and then recruit another juvenile to assist in the theft. The two young juveniles would then stake out an ATM and wait for a potential victim to approach the ATM. When the suspect spotted a potential victim making a transaction or withdrawal at the ATM, the suspect would quickly approach the victim at the ATM and ask them if they wanted to purchase some candy. Because of the suspect's quick approach and loud voice, the victims were startled and, at first, thought they were being robbed. All of the victims told the suspect no, grabbed their currency from the ATM, and then quickly walked away from the ATM to their vehicle. Because the suspect had scared the victims so much, they had forgotten to remove their debit card or credit card from the Automated Teller Machine. After each ATM transaction, the machine usually asks you if you want another transaction. The suspect, in these cases, pressed yes and then punched in the amount of a subsequent withdrawal from the victim's account. After making as many transactions as he could, the suspect then removed the debit card or credit card from the machine and used the card making credit transactions at stores and other locations.

This particular suspect was very experienced in this type of fraudulent activity and used this particular approach for about eight more years. He was apprehended several times as a juvenile and also as an adult offender. I arrested the suspect several years later after he had completed the same scam and was attempting to use the stolen credit card at an area merchant. The victim had notified the financial institution and the card had been reported as stolen. The suspect attempted to make a purchase at the business and the loss prevention manager was notified of the incident. As luck would have it, I was not far away from the business when the loss prevention manager notified me. Upon my arrival at the location, the loss prevention manager and I approached the suspect. The suspect recognized me from earlier incidents and immediately attempted to run away. After a short foot pursuit and a fight, the suspect was apprehended. His accomplice, waiting outside in a parked vehicle, was able to get away. The suspect was arrested and charged accordingly. He didn't get much jail time though because after each arrest, the suspect would always request another detective stating that he had information pertaining to a violent crime. The suspect did have a vast knowledge of criminal activity and would give the detective and prosecuting attorney what they needed to make a case on a violent crime in exchange for a lenient sentence for his criminal acts. The suspect continued to play this until he was apprehended by another jurisdiction which did not make deals. The last that I heard, the suspect was serving hard time.

ATMs can be the site of the actual crime as in the aforementioned paragraph, a robbery, or perhaps the sneaky fraud perpetrator's skimming device. We had investigated several incidents involving thefts from Automated Teller Machines. One such fraudulent theft involved the suspects using different means to disable the Automated Teller Machine so that the victim's debit card or credit card would get stuck inside of the machine. The victim would eventually give up attempting to retrieve their debit card or credit card and leave the location. After the victim left the ATM, the suspect or suspects would go to the location of the ATM and remove the victim's card. The suspect(s) would then take the card and immediately begin to make fraudulent transactions.

Credit card skimmers have also been known to place portable skimming devices on the front of ATMs. Remarkably, some of the devices look like the actual machine and only a trained eye can tell the difference. We had several such skimming devices placed on ATMs throughout the city of Atlanta. The skimming devices were placed over the machine's card insert and whenever a victim made a transaction, their debit card or credit card was skimmed and the information contained thereupon was saved. The victims inserted their card, made their transaction, and then retrieved their card without ever knowing that the card's information had been stolen. Most of the cases that we encountered dealt only with the skimming device being placed over the card insert opening; however, the fraud perpetrator has been able to capture an individual's P.I.N. or Personal Identification Number also. The fraud perpetrator will enable the use of small hidden cameras focused at the ATMs keyboard or they will place a fake keyboard on top of the ATMs keyboard. These modern days fraud perpetrators are head and shoulders above the fraud perpetrators of years past. In the beginning, fraud perpetrators made a large metal and plastic box and placed it on the ATM. These large boxes did not look anything like the original machine but, as usually, did fool some people. As the fraud perpetrator became more and more knowledgeable, so did their ability to build skimming devices which looked like part of the original ATM and capable of going undetected for some time capturing hundreds of credit card and debit card numbers and information.

Whenever you are using an ATM, be aware of your surroundings and be alert. If, by chance, someone does approach you in a quick and startling way, be sure to remove your debit card or credit card from the machine along with your currency. As for skimming devices, look at ATMs that you have used in the past and acquaint yourself with their appearance. If something looks out of place, contact the financial institution's security department and report the machine. A qualified person or law enforcement officer will respond to the location and investigate.

Chapter Ten

Internet Loan Scams and Advanced Fee Scams

I recently worked an extremely large case involving more than 100 victims across the nation. Actually, that is the number of victims who had fallen prey to an advanced fee loan scam. In my opinion, the number of victims will never truly be known because I could never really discover exactly how many victims actually applied for a loan with their personal and financial identifiers but stopped short of actually sending the perpetrators money. It is always a crime when someone obtains and/or records your personal and financial identifiers without your permission or if the means were fraudulent in the very first place such as this case. This information is a commodity in today's underworld of deceit and fraud. We have discovered that personal information and financial information is sold and traded for drugs, sex, vehicles, and electronic items such as laptops, cellular telephones, etc.

The scam was very well orchestrated and planned. First, the perpetrators obtained a web site. The web site was designed in such a fashion that it appeared to be a legitimate business. The web site consisted of several pages which included an application page. The so-called business claimed to be located at a prestigious address in Atlanta, Georgia and actually had a picture of the business complex in their advertisement.

Most of the victims who applied to this bogus web site were doing so to consolidate high interest credit card debts, purchase or repair a vehicle or motorcycle, or pay off an outstanding hospital debt. Victims would search the internet for loans or personal loans and would find the bogus website. The site offered non-secured personal loans of just about any amount at a 7% interest rate and people having any type of credit, good or bad, could obtain a loan. The home page of this site included eligibility requirements which read that to obtain a loan all you had to do was be a U.S. citizen, be eighteen years of age or older, and earn at least $12,000 per year. The application page, which by the way was not a secure page, requested that the victim give their name, address, date of birth, social security number, telephone numbers of home and at work, employer data, and length of time at their present employer.

After submitting their applications, all of the victims were contacted either by email or telephone advising them that they had been approved for their personal loan but that there was a problem with their credit. A lot of people across the nation have some type of problem with their credit history, whether it is a late payment or too much debt so it is not surprising that this worked. All of the victims were told that in order to obtain their non-secured personal loan that they would have to remit a "down payment" in the amount of 10 percent of their loan amount. The perpetrators made the victims believe that this down payment was a requirement and even went as far as sending one victim an email stating that the company's insurance would cover up to 90 percent of the loan value so therefore, they needed the additional 10 percent. The victims were also told that this down payment would be held and only used in case of a default in the repayment of the loan.

The victims were all required to fax additional documents to the perpetrators which contained even more personal and financial information of the victim such as loan amounts and what the loans were for. After receiving the aforementioned information, the perpetrators told each victim to wire transfer their down payment to a person. When the victim questioned this, the perpetrators would tell each victim that this person was a security officer of the company or that this person was now their loan officer. The victims were also asked to give their checking account information such as routing numbers and account numbers. The suspects told each victim that after the business had received their down payments that their loan would be wired directly into their checking account within 24 to 48 hours. After the two days had passed and no funds had been transferred into the victim's accounts, the victims attempted to contact the suspects to no avail. All of these victims were now out their hard earned or even borrowed funds plus whatever fees they incurred to conduct the wire transfer.

I first became aware of this fraudulent internet business while working on another case in my office one late afternoon. A lady, from Oregon, called the office inquiring about the business and said that she and her husband had applied for a $20,000 personal loan and had been told that they were approved but because of their credit, they had to submit a $2,000 down payment. I immediately began an investigation. I soon discovered that the business did not exist at the location that they advertised and that the Georgia Department of Banking and Finance, which regulates all lenders who have a physical address in the state of Georgia, did not have any record of that particular business. The state did have a record on a small mortgage company in South Georgia by that name but that business did not have any locations in or around Atlanta, did not offer personal loans of any type, and did not have a web site.

As I was searching the World Wide Web, I discovered that several people had gone to an internet question board inquiring about the business. I responded to one of the questions asking the person to call me at the Major Fraud office. After that, our office became swamped with calls from victims all across the United States. I attempted to answer each and every call and advise each victim to place a verbal and extended fraud alert on their credit profile, fax or email their documents with a statement to the fraud office, and file a complaint with the Federal Trade Commission. As time went by, we had victims from all walks of life. We had fellow law enforcement Officers, loan officers, banking employees, United States Military personnel, and individuals who basically worked very hard for a living. It really got to me, speaking with as many of the victims that I could and still conduct an extremely hard and wearisome investigation. These were not victims who were looking to cash in on a get rich scheme but each one was just trying to obtain a loan that would enable them to live life a little bit easier. This case definitely affected my outlook on life and eventually my career. One of the victims happened to suffer from a hearing impairment and needed the use of a computer assisted translator to file the police report. This was especially disturbing to me because the perpetrators knew this and still took advantage anyway. I often wonder what type of rock this creature or shall I say creatures, plural, crawled out from underneath. Needless to say, I didn't just want to arrest these pieces of shit but I wanted to give them the ass beating of their life.

As the case progressed and the number of victims grew, so did the number of bogus and fraudulent web sites that these suspects operated. Within one month, during the investigation, two additional fraudulent web sites were up and running. Since a lot of victims were going to internet question and answer boards, the perpetrators decided that they would set up additional sites with different business names. The second site which appeared also claimed to be located in the city of Atlanta. The location exists; however, no such business ever was located inside of the complex. The second web site was a mirror image of the first web site; only the name and address were changed. The application was the same.

The third web site was, without a doubt, the perpetrators best designed site. It added testimonials with an enhanced application page. This business also claimed to be located at one of Atlanta's premier business complexes and had the picture of the complex on the contact page.

This was extremely frustrating. Now, I had three bogus web sites and only could guess that more were coming. Each and every day, we were receiving calls from new victims and victims calling to check in on the investigation. I tried for three months to get someone to obtain a civil order to have these sites shut down and removed. My partner, Detective P.E.Cooper, who is without a doubt the best fraud detective I have ever had the pleasure to have known, was the person responsible for getting the sites shut down. While at my desk, he came by and asked if anyone had contacted the hosts for the sites. I had generated subpoenas to the sites for information but never thought to ask the hosts if they would remove the sites without a civil order. Detective Cooper jumped right in and contacted each host explaining that each site was completely fraudulent and requested that they be removed immediately. Detective Cooper was able to accomplish in a matter of hours what I had been trying to do for three months.

I was able to tie each of these fraudulent web sites to the same people because of their M.O. or Modus Operandi. All three web sites operated in the same manner and all of the documents had the same format.

The security officers or loan officers of the business were the individuals that the victims had wired the funds to. I traced these people and began making arrests of these suspects because of their part in the crime. These individuals were recruited to go in to wire transfer locations and retrieve the funds. These suspects would exit the business and then give the funds to the middle man who recruited them. At the end of the day and after picking up several wire transfers, they were given a share of the funds. I was surprised to find out that these runners or mules only received $40 or $50 per day. Often with fraud perpetrators and their mules, the fraud perpetrator will give the mule about a fifth or a quarter of the proceeds. These mules were picking up between $500 and $3,000 each pickup and were doing multiple pickups each and every day.

By the time of my retirement, I had arrested three of the mules, had outstanding felony warrants on five others, and had positively identified the middle man who had recruited the mules. All of the suspects were charged with Racketeer Influenced and Corrupt Organizations or RICO, Identity Fraud, Theft by Deception, Computer Theft, and Conspiracy to Commit a Crime. I was bound and determined that every person taking part in this elaborate fraudulent enterprise would, at least, be charged with the maximum charges within my power.

This case pushed me to the point of mental and physical exhaustion. It was a case that I was damn proud to have worked but it was the case that eventually caused my early retirement. All of my career, I treated people with respect and dignity even though some of their actions and crimes made my stomach turn. As I worked this case though, I felt myself changing. I wanted to really hurt the people that I was chasing because of what they had done and what they were doing to honest, hard working people. I guess the fact that in just about every step of the investigation I was met with businesses either refusing to cooperate with the investigation or that they needed paper or a subpoena to produce what I needed did not help the situation. I believe that I typed more subpoenas on this case than all of the other cases in my career.

The problem with subpoenas is time. A detective will type the subpoena requesting information pertinent to the case and then wait for the evidence to come back. Some companies allow you to fax a subpoena; however, several companies require the subpoena to be mailed. Once the business receives the subpoena, it may be a month or two months before the detective actually has the evidence he or she needs. To make matters worse, many businesses in other states do not recognize subpoenas outside of their own state. This has always bothered me because subpoenas are a court order. Businesses often thumb their noses at law enforcement and the courts. I have never had a problem with a business requiring a subpoena for the production of evidence except for the time factor in which they get the information to you. I swear, especially in this particular case, it seemed that several businesses were more interested in protecting the perpetrators instead of helping hundreds of victims across the United States.

For example, during the investigation several telephone numbers came up. I was trying to locate the provider of one such number and I knew that many telephone numbers have been ported out to another company. A lot of law enforcement resources are now outdated and the one that I was using was often misleading. From a detective's point of view, if you have to submit a subpoena to someone for evidence it is always smart to submit it to the right business from the start. I called the telephone company inquiring if the number was theirs or if it had been ported out to another company. The investigator on the other end of the line told me that I needed to submit a subpoena first. Now, this is totally incorrect. A subpoena is only needed when law enforcement is seeking personal information about a party. It is not needed to find out what particular telephone company services a telephone number. I immediately hung up the telephone and called the security director for the telephone company and got the information that I needed. This saved about a month of the investigation. If I had submitted a subpoena to that business, I would have been informed about a month later that they did not service that number anymore and I would have to contact the current provider.

As the number of mules increased, the more subpoenas were sent. As each subpoena returned, it generated more requests for evidence for new information. These perpetrators took great lengths to cover their tracks but were not completely successful.

I did incur a problem with an area check cashing business where some of the perpetrators picked up wire transfers. First, the business did not possess any working video surveillance equipment so obtaining video surveillance photographs was impossible. Second, the business refused my initial subpoena for the production of evidence which consisted of the receipts the perpetrator had signed and touched. These were crucial to the investigation. I went to the location, subpoena in hand, accompanied by two United States Secret Service Special Agents to retrieve the evidence. The store manager refused to give the evidence to me and their legal department advised that someone from the business would appear at the Grand Jury with the evidence. Needless to say, no one from the business came to the Grand Jury and I did not receive the evidence that I needed. I went back to the business and they told me that they had mailed copies of the receipts. This was totally unacceptable. I required the first generation or original receipts not copies of the receipts. I pretty much pitched a temper tantrum in the store. When I got back to the office, I was still steaming. After I left the business, the manager notified the business' legal department. I received a telephone call from their legal department not long after my arrival at the major fraud office. My statement was quick and to the point. I advised the corporate attorney that I was through playing games with them. I would no longer submit a subpoena for the production of evidence. I would, however, enter the business armed with a search warrant, shut the business down until I got the evidence, and arrest anyone who obstructed justice. The attorney immediately contacted the wire company. Within one hour, the attorney called back informing me that I would not have any more problems obtaining evidence from any of their locations. It is always a shame when someone, such as a law enforcement officer trying to help others, has to jump through hoops to get the necessary evidence. It probably would not have bothered me as bad, but several of these businesses knew that people were being taken in great numbers because the victims had been filing complaints with them also and yet they were still hesitant to assist.

There were a lot of red flags that started to appear as I began investigating this case. The site's application was not secure. Normally, if you go to a legitimate banker or lender's site it will redirect you to a more secure site so that whatever you transmit cannot be captured by anyone. The second red flag appeared when the suspect told the victims that they had been approved but since there was a problem with their credit, they needed to submit a 10 percent down payment to receive their loan. This is illegal, period. Whether it is called an advance fee, down payment, or any other term they might come up with, the bottom line it is illegal. Down payments are legal when you are purchasing tangible property such as a vehicle, motorcycle, boat, or real estate. But think about it, you are putting 10% to 20% down, the bank or lender is putting in the other 80% to 90% and you are walking away with the item with an agreement that you will repay the lender the amount of the loan plus interest. Certain loans do carry fees but these fees are almost always deducted from the note. Legitimate lenders will never ask you for a down payment on a personal loan.

The World Wide Web is a great tool for everyone. It is like having a library in your own home and also provides the convenience of shopping without the hassle of fighting traffic and enables you to locate a wide range of products and services that you might not otherwise be able to locate. As with just about everything else though, the fraud perpetrators have also discovered this and using this to their advantage. The Free Enterprise system is basically a system designed on trust. You make a purchase using a check or credit card or perhaps take out a loan, it is trust that allows the seller or the lender to allow you to make that purchase or give you that loan on the understanding that your check will be good or that you promise to repay the loan.

How can you detect an internet loan scam and prevent becoming a victim? First, I would always recommend going to the financial institution where you conduct most of your personal business. Second, if you do seek a loan and wish to use the World Wide Web to help facilitate this loan, I would recommend that you fully investigate the loan site. A lot of victims in this case contacted the Better Business Bureau before they sent their money to the suspects. The BBB report for these three loan sites revealed that they were not a member of the BBB and the BBB had no complaints on them within the last 36 months. That was in the beginning when the sites first appeared and could not reveal any past complaints because the scam sites did not have any to that date. It is important to remember that these web sites are set up to take as many people as possible in a very, very short time. Their scam only works until word gets out. After that, the scam does not work because people do not apply. The BBB has a totally different report on these three loan sites now. The majority of businesses, legitimate businesses, do belong to the BBB. One of the victims did inquire as to why the scam business was not a member and the suspect told her that is part of the way they keep their costs down. Total bull shit. If the business is not a member of the BBB, it may be an indicator that the business is not legitimate.

One thing to watch out for is the fact that many perpetrators are incorporating their bogus and fraudulent businesses with a Secretary of State's office prior to committing any criminal acts. This makes their fraudulent business seem more legitimate. Businesses can be incorporated through the internet and fraud perpetrators often use stolen identities to help facilitate this action. So just because you search the Secretary of State's web site and discover that the business is registered with the Secretary of State, do not take for granted that it is legitimate.

Before you ever apply, I would recommend that you first call the business and request that they send you a copy of the loan documents. Read the fine print. I would also recommend researching the location of the business. In this particular case, the fraudulent businesses claimed to be located at three prestigious addresses in Atlanta, Georgia however none of the complexes had any tenant even resembling those businesses. If you are still in doubt as to whether you are dealing with a legitimate lender or not, contact that state's Department of Banking and Finance. Lenders are regulated and it is mandatory that they be registered as such with the Department of Banking and Finance. If the Department of Banking and Finance does not have a record of the business at that address, you have probably discovered a fraudulent business. If you suspect that you have discovered a fraudulent business or web site, contact the police department which has jurisdiction of the location that the business claims to be located and file a report. I also recommend that you file a report with the Federal Trade Commission and the National White Collar Crime Center or NW3C.

Chapter Eleven

Internet Auctions

Internet auctions can be a fantastic place to purchase items and often you can get a great deal on a lot of items that you might have trouble locating anywhere else. As I have mentioned before, the fraud perpetrators find a way to ruin it for a lot of people. People have often heard the expression, let the buyer beware but in today's world of fraud the seller needs to stay alert also. I will try to cover some of the scams and cons that modern day fraud perpetrators use whenever they use online auction houses to facilitate their criminal activities. Online auction houses attempt to rid their sites of any fraud; however, it is extremely difficult when they are dealing with millions of people each and every day. The fraud perpetrator is imaginative and will often change names, passwords, computers, etc. to continue their criminal activities.

There are several scenarios regarding online fraud activities. Often the fraud victim will order an item online, pay for the item, and then never receive the item or when the item arrives it will not be exactly as it was advertised. Online auction houses usually have some type of guarantee that allows for the customer to receive part, if not all, of their payment back.

One thing, to be extremely mindful of, whenever ordering or purchasing items or merchandise is to watch out for the counterfeit products. Counterfeit merchandise such as name brand clothing, sports jerseys, watches, eyewear, jewelry, hand bags, and wallets are among some of the more popular items which fraud perpetrators sell in flea markets and online auctions. The fraud perpetrator is able to offer these items at a price usually less that half of what the originals would sell for. Counterfeiters have gotten extremely accurate in a lot of their reproductions and sometimes it is difficult to tell the difference between the original product and the counterfeit product without the assistance of someone trained in that field.

The biggest losses occur to the people who are purchasing a vehicle or motorcycle. In one case, the fraud perpetrator took pictures of a vehicle which was being sold on a dealer's lot, the vehicle identification number off of another similar vehicle, and then posted the car for auction. The seller had listed an address in Atlanta and had instructed the winner of the sale to wire the funds to his account. After the victim wired the funds, he never received the vehicle. The victim filed a police report and I conducted the investigation with the assistance of the auction's investigator and the investigator for the insurance company. The victim filed a police report with the Atlanta Police Department because the address of the suspect was listed as an Atlanta address. After investigating this incident, it was discovered that the address did not exist but I investigated the case until I could no longer proceed. The wire transfer was actually received in New York and the suspect made several withdrawals in New York immediately after receiving the funds. Since I couldn't fly up to New York and continue the investigation, I was forced to forward the case to the agency with jurisdiction in New York. This is often a problem that fraud detectives face whenever faced with crimes that involve wire transfers. The suspect will list an address which is fake or wrong; however, it is the only point to begin the investigation. Police agencies have certain venues or areas that they can investigate, arrest, and charge a suspect for a particular crime. If the crime occurred in another jurisdiction, I could arrest the suspect and turn him or her over to that jurisdiction and they would proceed in charging and prosecuting the suspect. In most cases, venue is often dictated by the perpetrator's location. In this case, that happened to be in New York.

Probably the most intriguing case that I worked regarding online auctions was a case that involved a second chance purchase. The victim had bid on a motorcycle which had been listed for auction. The bike carried a reserve price which meant that the seller did not have to sell the bike if that price was not met. If the reserve is met or goes beyond the reserve, the seller is obligated to sell the item to the highest bidder. In this case, however, the reserve was not met and the seller did not sell the bike. The victim received an email, which appeared to be from the online auction, asking him if he still wanted to purchase the bike for his bid of $16,500. This was quite a deal and the victim emailed back stating that he would purchase the bike. The victim received another email with instructions to wire transfer the $16,500. After about a week, the victim had not received the bike. He had made several attempts to contact the seller but was unsuccessful. Realizing that he had been taken, he came to the fraud office and filed a police report. I requested that he print all of the emails that he had received and forward them to me.

As the case was proceeding, the victim began to investigate the case also. He was a firm believer that the seller had taken his money and not given him his property. This case was extremely unusual because, as it turned out, both the buyer/victim and the seller lived in Atlanta. The victim, through his own investigation, found out exactly where the seller lived and even took photographs of the bike which had been parked outside. As I continued the investigation though, I was uncertain of the validity of the emails the victim had received.

Second chance offers do exist on items with a reserve, however it is completely left up to the seller, and the online auction will keep a record of all second chance offerings. The investigators for the online auction confirmed that the seller did not offer any second chance auction and no record existed. I contacted the seller and interviewed him concerning the incident. The seller stated that he had never offered any second chance on his bike and that he had been contacted by two other people inquiring if the second chance offer was for real. It became evident that my victim was the victim of an elaborate phishing scam. The wire transfer had been received in Maryland and the fraud suspect immediately made withdrawals from the account. Once again, I was forced to forward the case to the jurisdiction with venue. The fraud suspects in this case were able to set up a phishing email which resembled the auction's page and they sent this email to several people who had placed bids on the bike. This is a prime example of the working minds of the fraud perpetrators. At times, they are extremely imaginative and creative.

I have purchased items through online auctions and have had great success. Whenever I purchase a small item, for say less than $100.00, I pay for the items through the auction house pay site. I understand that I could become a victim also and I am taking a chance. I do look at how long the seller has been a member and what their approval rating is. I also research what type of items he or she has sold in the past. I usually do not bother with the item if the seller's approval rating is not above 99 percent or they have not had a lot of prior transactions.

Whenever you are purchasing large and/or expensive items such as vehicles, motorcycles, boats, machinery, and jewelry, I highly recommend that you look at the item before making your purchase. This may limit what you are able to purchase but it could save you a lot of money in the long run. Avoid any sales that require you to wire transfer the funds into an account. Fraud perpetrators love the wire transfer. They can tell the victim that they are located somewhere but actually be located in some other state or even another country. By the time the detective works the case and gets information on the wire transfer back, it could be a month or so later.

Individuals and businesses offering merchandise for sale should also be aware of the fraud perpetrator. Fraud perpetrators will often purchase items using counterfeit checks. If you are a seller of an item and someone sends you a personal check, cashier's check, or money order, you should take that check or money order to your banking institution and have it verified before cashing it or depositing it into your account. I know that, even in today's times, customer satisfaction still exists at numerous businesses and these businesses attempt to please the customer in every way. I would recommend that before shipping any item always verify the funds first.

Chapter Twelve

The Pet Scam

A few years back, Detective P.E.Cooper and I worked a heart breaking case. The Fraud office began receiving reports from victims who had stated that they had lost a pet and someone, in the Atlanta area, had contacted them saying that they had found their lost animal. The victims were all reporting that they had wired the suspect money for the return of the animal but never received the pet back. All in all, I guess we had over fifteen such reports.

Detective Cooper and I compiled all of the cases that we had on this suspect and went to work. After speaking with several of the victims and learning how the suspect had not only scammed them out of money but had played with their emotions while doing so, we decided to concentrate on this particular case until it was solved.

All of our victims in this case were residents of other states, many of which surrounded the state of Georgia. The victims offered a reward for the return of their dog and placed an advertisement in the lost and found section of their local newspaper. After placing the advertisement, the victims were all contacted by a male claiming that he was a long haul truck driver and while traveling through their area, he saw an injured animal on the side of the highway. The suspect definitely had the gift of gab and would communicate with each victim for hours on end while he was working the scam. Through tactical and imaginative communication, he was able to have the victim fully describe their lost pet and then turn this information to his advantage.

After the initial telephone call to the victim, the suspect had them convinced that he did, indeed, have their lost pet. He would always tell them that the pet had been injured and that he had paid for the veterinarian expenses but always reassured the victim that the animal was okay and now in good health. The suspect would then offer to ship the pet back to the owner via an airline but told the victim that he did not have a carrier for the animal or that his carrier was not big enough and he needed to go out and purchase another one. Of course, all of the good hearted, honest, and hard working victims offered to reimburse all of his expenses and send him the money for a new carrier. The suspect would play the scam to the tilt and upon the victim's insistence would agree to accept the payment to cover the pet's medical expenses, carrier cost, and shipping charges. The suspect would then tell the victims to wire the funds to him in the name he had given them which was an alias. The victims wired the funds and the suspect received those funds at businesses in and around Atlanta. After receiving the funds though, the suspect did not stop the scam. He would then call the victims back and advise them that he had shipped their pet via the airline and would go in to detail as what airline, departure, and arrival time at their nearest airport. The victims drove their local airport and waited for their pet to arrive on the scheduled flight. You can imagine the heartbreak when the flights arrived but the victims found out that their pet was not onboard.

Detective Cooper generated a subpoena for the production of evidence for all of the wire transfers that the suspect had received. We drove to every location retrieving all available video surveillance photographs and interviewing the employees of the businesses who had served the suspect. The name that the suspect had used as an alias was a very common name and because of the wire transfers, no other identifiable information was available. We did now know the physical characteristics of the suspect, through the video surveillance footage, but had no idea who he was.

The Good Lord does work in mysterious ways. As we were stumped investigating this case, we got a couple of huge breaks. The first came when a victim reporting the same crime told us that she had made two wire transfers to the suspect for the return of her lost pet. The suspect had given the victim an alias name on the first wire transfer but had called her back to tell her that his carrier was not large enough to ship the animal and that he had to wait until he got his paycheck to purchase another larger carrier. The victim agreed to pay for the larger carrier so that she could get her pet back quicker and wired a second transfer to the suspect. The suspect slipped up on this one though, he told the victim to wire the money to someone else using his real identity. When the victim questioned this, the suspect quickly recovered and told her that this person was his cousin.

Our second break in the case came when Detective Cooper and I were contacted by a detective in Florida. This detective is an extremely excellent investigator. He had called the fraud office and had spoken with Detective Cooper and me about the case. He said that he was working an A.P.E. case and needed our assistance. As he began to explain the case, Detective Cooper and I each asked if the pet was a monkey and he laughed. He explained that an A.P.E. case was an acronym for an Acute Political Emergency. He went on to explain that the owner of the lost pet was a very close friend of someone very high in political office and that they had been scammed by our suspect. The victim was able to obtain information which this detective was able to trace to our suspect. These pieces of evidence enabled law enforcement to concentrate on the suspect instead of chasing aliases.

Detective Cooper then, through a series of investigative maneuvers and searches, found all of the other identifiable information on the suspect. The suspect had been arrested, convicted, and served time in a Texas state prison for fraud. He had been paroled and placed on probation less than a year earlier. He had relocated to Georgia and was residing in a half way house just west of Atlanta. Detective Cooper obtained warrants for the suspect's arrest and we drove to the location. Upon our arrival though, we discovered that the suspect had been released from probation the middle of November and was no longer living at the location. The manager of the house said that as a condition of their probation, all probationers had to obtain and keep gainful employment. She pulled the suspect's records and gave us the location of the business that the suspect had been employed with while he stayed at the half way house. The employment choice of our suspect was a telemarketer.

Detective Cooper and I left the half way house on our way to the telemarketing business. When we arrived at the location, we explained that we had arrest warrants for the suspect. The manager was extremely helpful but said that the suspect had terminated his employment in December and his last known address was the half way house. Boom, we were stumped again. We now knew who to look for but finding him, in a metropolitan area containing over 5 million people, would not be easy. As we were about to leave the business, a secretary who just came back from lunch asked me what the Atlanta Police were doing there. I told her that we were looking for one of their ex-employees by the name of so and so. She looked astonished and told me that she had received a fax from him yesterday requesting that his W-2's be mailed to his new address of 2625 Piedmont Road NE, Atlanta, Georgia.

Detective Cooper and I each knew that 2625 Piedmont Road NE was not an apartment complex but a strip mall containing several businesses and restaurants. One of the businesses, though, was a mail drop business. We entered the business and spoke with the manager who told us that the suspect had leased a Post Office Box at the location for a period of six months and that he comes in every two or three days to pick up his mail. We gave the manager our number and told him to call us the next time the suspect came in to the business.

As we got into our vehicle, I told Detective Cooper that the suspect had to be close. We suspected that he did not drive because he did not have any form of transportation at the half way house. Therefore, I reasoned that he must be within walking distance of the mail drop. There are about a dozen or so apartment complexes within walking distance of this business but I believed that the suspect might be staying in an extended stay hotel nearby. There were approximately three or four extended stay hotels within walking distance of the business. We decided to check them first.

We drove to the first extended stay hotel and spoke with the manager and the off duty Atlanta Officer providing security for the complex. The manager checked his roster and discovered that a person by our suspect's name was staying at the hotel and had been there several weeks. Detective Cooper and I went to the room and discovered the suspect still in bed. We gained entry and arrested him without incident.

The suspect was advised his Constitutional Rights but decided to waive those Rights and speak with us without an attorney present. Normally, I was always the one playing the good cop in the good cop, bad cop routine. In this case, I just couldn't pretend to befriend someone like this person. This individual had a way with words and had been very well educated. He told us that he had trouble with face to face confrontations but could communicate with others very well on the telephone. He told us that he was sorry for what he had done and said that he only did it so that he could live and eat. He went on to describe how he had heard about the scam about 15 years earlier and when he got down and out, decided to give it a try. After it worked, he kept going and going. He stated that he would search the World Wide Web for newspapers around the southeastern United States and search the lost and found in their classified section. Once he located a victim, he would research the area where the victim lived taking notes on specific businesses and other locations near by. He would learn the highways and interstates which ran through or nearby their location. He told us that he would get the victim to describe their lost animal and then use that information against the victim later on in their initial conversation. The victims were usually so happy that their lost pet had been found that they completely forgot that they had already told him everything he needed to know about the animal. When Detective Cooper asked him why he kept calling each of his victims even after receiving the wire transfers, he replied that he was lonely and he felt like these people were his friends.

It is very easy to become victimized whenever your emotions come into play. When emotions play a part, the scam artist knows that the victim does not have their guard up. Although cases such as this are rare, it is important for everyone to stop and think. You know that you want to believe that this stranger has something that belongs to you and that you love. Be careful as to what you tell the person about the lost animal or object. Let him or her tell you about the pet or lost object and make sure that he or she is very specific. Most lost animals are recovered somewhere near the owner's home. If someone calls you from a long way off and tells you that they have recovered your lost pet, be careful. When we questioned the suspect as to why he didn't do any scams involving people from Georgia, he quickly stated that the scam would not work because the victim always wanted to drive to Atlanta and pick up the animal personally.

The suspect did not scam the victims for a lot of money in this case. If it had been a case of check fraud, credit card fraud, or simple theft by conversion, this suspect would have probably received probation. But because the suspect played with the emotions of a lot of people, he received a lengthy jail sentence.

Chapter Thirteen

Slick and Quick

When I was working patrol in the business district of Atlanta several years ago, we had a large problem with someone stealing money from cash registers in stores and businesses. The Asset Protection Manager of one large department store had several of these thefts and, at first, suspected employees of the thefts. But stores, especially large retail stores with asset protection employees, are very careful and much like a police agency will develop Probable Cause before accusing or detaining a person. The Asset Protection Manager diligently reviewed hours and hours of video surveillance footage before finally finding her perpetrator.

The surveillance video revealed what the suspect looked like and a BOLO or be on the lookout for was sent to every one of the stores in the chain. About a week or so later, the Asset Protection Manager spotted the suspect coming back in to the store and as watchful eyes and video surveillance cameras followed him; he skillfully opened a locked but unmanned cash register, took the currency out, and placed it inside of his pants pocket. The suspect was apprehended as he was attempting to leave the business and arrested for the crime. Warrants were obtained on previous occasions of theft which we could prove through the video surveillance. The suspect did not receive much jail time and was back out on the streets within a few months.

A few years later, after I had made detective, I began receiving several reports of employee thefts. The reports were all pretty much the same, employee suspected of stealing currency out of the cash register. Some reports just reported money stolen from register without any suspect information. I began to wonder if the individual that I had arrested years earlier was back in town and at it again. I went back and pulled the police reports from the individual's previous arrest, obtained his booking photographs, and contacted the Asset Protection Manager who had initially discovered this guy.

As I began investigating the present incidents, I went to the stores and spoke with the managers and loss prevention employees, if that store employed any. A lot of these stores did not possess any type of video surveillance equipment so trying to build a concrete shut case was just about impossible. Of the several stores that reported the thefts, only about two had any type of video surveillance equipment. I had the managers and loss prevention employees research the video surveillance tapes for anyone near the register from which the currency had been stolen. This was a time consuming task for each of the two businesses because they did not know the exact time of the incidents. They did know that the crimes had occurred between the hour of one day and the date and time when the theft was discovered.

After a period of searching, the managers and loss prevention employees notified me that they had discovered an individual standing in front of the register and described the individual as an older male. I drove to each of the stores and obtained the video surveillance tapes. I reviewed the tapes in my office and compared them with the suspect's booking photographs. No doubt, I had positively identified my suspect and began typing arrest warrants for his arrest.

After obtaining arrest warrants for this suspect, I began to try to locate him in an area populated by millions of people. The suspect did not possess a valid driver's license nor did he have a recent identification card, so finding an address to begin was difficult. On a hunch, I began to check with the extended stay hotels in the area. As luck would have it, I located the suspect in an extended stay hotel not very far away from the locations where the incidents had occurred.

Instead of executing the arrest warrants for the suspect right away, I decided that I needed the keys which the suspect possessed to be able to tie all of his criminal activities together. I drew up a search warrant and the affidavit and took it to Superior Court. After obtaining the signed search warrant, I proceeded to the extended stay hotel to exact the arrest and conduct a search of the room.

The suspect's arrest went down without incident and inside of the hotel room; I found what I had obtained the search warrant for. The suspect had a key ring full of keys and many of those keys were cash register keys. Needless to say, the suspect was not happy to see me. After advising him of his Constitutional Rights, I asked him if he wanted to speak with me regarding any of the incidents. He immediately replied "No, I have nothing to say to you."

We relocated the suspect and evidence to our office so that I could finish my paperwork. While we were driving to the office, we passed two of the businesses that the suspect had stolen money from. I was in the back seat of the vehicle with the suspect and made the comment that he had hit those two stores. The suspect just looked at me and didn't say a word. As we kept driving, I told the suspect that he was one of the best I had ever seen and that I was impressed with how he was able to do all of this and go undetected.

When we arrived at my office, I sat the suspect next to my desk and began typing the arrest report. As I was typing the report, the suspect turned to me and said, "Detective, I believe that I will talk to you." I stopped typing the report and started debriefing the suspect.

I knew the M.O. or Modus Operandi of this guy but I was shocked to find out the true extent of his crimes. The suspect was usually accompanied by his girlfriend and the two of them would enter a business. The girlfriend would usually make a small purchase. Often, the trick was to pick a cash register operated by the store's employee to purchase the girlfriend's items which was right next to a cash register which was unmanned and locked. As his girlfriend would be paying for her merchandise, the suspect would back up to the unmanned register. With his back to the cash register, the suspect would remove the cash register key from his pants pocket, locate the cash register's lock, and then unlock the register's drawer. He would allow the register's drawer to open about two or three inches using his rear to keep it from being noticed by anyone. He would then remove all of the currency inside of the register's drawer, place the currency in his pants pocket, shut the drawer, and then relock the drawer removing the key and placing it back into his pants pocket. He was so efficient at this method; he never had to look back behind him to complete any of the process. I asked the suspect how much he had stolen in his career. He paused for a moment and said "Well over a million dollars, I would get about $30,000 to $40,000 per year, enough to get by." I asked the suspect if he had ever worked anywhere and he replied "I didn't have to." The suspect told me that he would travel from location to location and never had to worry about spending money or living expenses. After his arrest, I was contacted by numerous jurisdictions in the southeast inquiring about his information and booking photographs because they had similar unsolved cases.

I often wonder how many employees were accused of stealing money from the cash registers. How many of them were fired and how many of them had been wrongly prosecuted for the thefts? It is important that law enforcement as well as store owners, managers, and loss prevention employees have all of the facts of the case before ever accusing anyone of any criminal activity. In cases such as this, it is impossible to make the case without quality video surveillance or the slight chance of someone witnessing the incident. A lot of businesses do not possess any type of surveillance equipment and those businesses suffer from crimes such as these.

Chapter Fourteen

The Lottery Ticket and Sweepstakes Scam

I have investigated numerous cases involving fraud related lottery tickets. A lot of individuals play the lottery hoping to find a quick cure for most of their money problems. Most people rarely win but for the lucky few that do win, they can now experience to purchase things that they had only dreamed of before. With each new lottery winner, the average lottery player is given more and more hope that he or she will also become a winner one day. Fraud perpetrators and con men use this hope to their advantage because they know that people will often drop their common sense and believe that their ship has arrived and their prayers have been answered.

Most of the cases which we encountered dealt with individuals receiving a letter in the mail. As the individual opened the letter, they discover that they are part winners in the Canadian Lottery or European Lottery. Usually the letter will contain a counterfeit check made payable to the individual. The counterfeit check varies in amounts however most are in the $4000 to $6000 range. The letter advises the individual that this check will be used to cover the expenses of recovering their lottery winnings which the suspect(s) advise is $150,000 to $250,000. They advise the individual to take the check to a financial institution, cash or deposit the check, and then wire transfer the funds back to the lottery organization or suspects. One very, very important thing to remember in anything is that in order to win something you must have first entered or played. I have never understood exactly why people want to believe that they had just won a lottery when they never played it in the first place. I guess people will often want it to be true that they drop their common senses. A lot of people receiving these lottery notices and checks will do exactly as the letter advises. They will promptly go to a financial institution and either deposit the check into their checking account or will attempt to cash the check outright.

Patrol officers and detectives have responded to financial institutions on calls that a person was inside attempting to cash a counterfeit check. When the officer or detective arrives at the scene, the individual is taken into custody and arrested for forgery. A lot of these individuals actually did not know that the check was counterfeit and, in one form or another, were victims also. They willfully, although not knowingly, committed a crime. If the individual is able to cash the counterfeit check, they then wire the funds to the perpetrators. Sometimes, the individual will deposit the check into his or her checking account, withdraw the funds, and then wire the funds to the fraud perpetrators. In both instances, the financial institution will be going after the individual to get their money back and in numerous cases file a police report and the police agency will commence an investigation. The individuals who fall for this scheme will very likely have to repay the banking institution and could run the risk of being arrested for a felony criminal act.

Cases such as lottery frauds are very hard to investigate because the perpetrators are almost always in another country. I have had a lot of people tell me that their wire transfer of the funds went to New York or California. One thing about wire transfers is that they can be picked up just about anywhere in the entire world. A destination must be listed at the time of the transfer but it is not something that is carved in stone, so to speak. A lot of these people thought they were wiring funds to people in the United States but actually the wire transfers were delivered to the fraud perpetrators residing in Canada, the United Kingdom, or other parts of the world.

People can prevent this from ever occurring just by using some plain and simple common sense. First, you can't win anything if you didn't play it in the first place. Second, why would someone send you a check for expenses, advise you to cash it, send the funds back to them, and then turn around and give you $150,000 or $250,000? As you can see, it just doesn't make any sense whatsoever. Don't let your wants and wishes overcome your common sense and get you into a lot of trouble.

Another case involving fraudulent lottery tickets actually involved two of the fraud perpetrators being present with the victims. The fraud perpetrators were actually very good con men with an unique scheme. The two fraud perpetrators, in this case, had done quite a bit of research on their intended victims and knew about how much money the victims had in their financial institution. It was a sad case, none the less, because the two victims actually lost their life savings to the two fraud perpetrators.

The scam began this way. The two victims of Middle Eastern decent worked very hard for their earnings. The two had come to the United States with the hope of starting a new life. They were working very hard and had saved their money hoping to purchase a home that they could live in and raise their family. The couple left their workplace and walked to a bus stop. As they sat waiting for their bus to take them home, another person walked up and sat down on the bench beside them. Soon after this person sat down on the bench, a Hispanic male approached the two victims and asked them if they knew how he could get to the lottery office. The Hispanic male began to explain that he had just won $60,000 by playing the lottery. The Hispanic male had a lottery ticket in his hand and acted very nervous. The two victims told the Hispanic male where the lottery office was located. The Hispanic male told the two victims that he was in the United States illegally and was afraid that when he claimed the winnings, he would be deported back to Mexico. The Hispanic male then offered the $60,000 ticket to the two victims for $20,000. The two victims told the Hispanic male that they didn't have that kind of money available. At that point, the other man sitting by the two victims, who had overheard everything, spoke. This individual told the two victims that he had $10,000 in his banking institution and if the two victims could put up the other $10,000 they could become partners and purchase the winning ticket from the Hispanic male. The two victims talked it over and decided that they would put their money in with that of the other man to buy the lottery ticket.

This other man told the victims that before buying the ticket they needed to check and see if the ticket was valid and indeed a winning ticket in the amount of $60,000. The four got up from the bus stop and then walked over to a parking area in front of a local convenience store. The unknown man told the Hispanic male and the two victims that he would take the lottery ticket inside of the convenience store and check the validity of the ticket. The Hispanic male gave the man the ticket and he walked inside of the convenience store while the victims and other male waited outside. After a few minutes, the man returned with the ticket and told the two victims that the ticket was real and was worth $60,000. The man then gave the lottery ticket back to the Hispanic male and told the two victims that he could drive them to their banking institution and his banking institution. This is the point where the victims should have expected something was terribly wrong. Why would a person be waiting on a bus, at a bus stop, when he had a drivable vehicle very near by? The victims ignored this fact and the four individuals got into the second suspect's vehicle. The suspect first drove to what he said was his banking institution, got out of the vehicle, and told the other three that he would return shortly. The suspect walked around the building, out of sight of the two victims, and returned a few minutes later with an envelope supposedly carrying currency. The suspect then drove to the two victims' banking institution and waited in the vehicle with the Hispanic male while the two victims went inside the financial institution and withdrew $10,000 from their savings. The suspect then drove back to the convenience store location near where they had first met. The suspect took his envelope and gave it to the Hispanic male. The two victims then took their envelope containing their savings and gave it to the Hispanic male. The Hispanic male then gave the other suspect the lottery ticket. This second suspect then gave the lottery ticket to the two victims and told them that he was going to drive the Hispanic male home and for them to wait for him, he would be back shortly. The two victims got out of the suspect's vehicle and the suspects drove away.

The two victims, being honest, waited an extremely long time for the other suspect to return. After this long wait, the two victims began to worry and became suspicious. The two then walked into the convenience store and presented the lottery ticket to the cashier for verification. To their surprise, the ticket was worthless. Imagine seeing all of your hard earned money disappear in a flash and dreams crumble. All the victims could provide law enforcement, in this case, were vague descriptions of the two suspects. Since the victims willfully withdrew their savings from the banking institution, the banking institution would not reimburse the funds. Their dream of owning their own home would now have to wait several more years. People have come to America to be free and live a life where they can follow their dreams and raise healthy and happy families. Crimes such as these are very heart breaking and sad.

Things to remember, in cases like these, are to use common sense. If something sounds too good to be true then it probably isn't true. Be especially mindful of things that require you to remove money from your savings and never be rushed into a decision concerning your future.

Chapter Fifteen

Mortgage Fraud

Probably one of the most lucrative frauds for the fraud perpetrator is residential mortgage fraud. The crime has become such a large problem that many states have enacted new laws which provide for the prosecution of these criminals. Residential mortgage fraud became such a problem in the state of Georgia; the State's Attorney General Office developed the first of such laws in the nation which was passed by the State's Legislature in 2005. At the time, Atlanta ranked number one in the nation for the crime. It was such a problem, that the Major Fraud Unit consisting of four detectives, at that time, had to devote two of these detectives full time to the investigation of mortgage fraud. Mortgage fraud does have a tremendous impact on a community and, if not stopped, can change a safe neighborhood into a run down, crime infested neighborhood practically overnight.

Mortgage fraud perpetrators can be various types. We have encountered people that are referred to as straw buyers, straw sellers, dishonest real estate appraisers, dishonest real estate agents, dishonest mortgage brokers, dishonest lending agents, and dishonest closing attorneys.

The straw buyer as they are referred is the person who is actually purchasing the property. The straw buyer does participate in the mortgage fraud; however, in most of the cases we have seen, the straw buyer can also be classified as a victim of another fraud perpetrator. The straw buyer is usually a person with a good credit score. The fraud perpetrators will seek these individuals and convince them that they can make a lot of money in real estate. As everyone knows, people have made a tremendous amount of money dealing in real estate. In the mortgage fraud, however, it is not the straw buyer making the money but the fraud perpetrator. The straw buyer is told that with their credit score, they will be able to purchase a residence. The fraud perpetrator will advise the straw buyer that they will arrange for all of the financing and after the purchase of the residence; they will find a renter for the property. The straw buyer is told that the renter will make the payments on the property and all they have to do is sit back and gain equity in the property.

Real estate transactions take place every day in America and most are legal. The mortgage fraud perpetrator does not deal in legal transactions. The fraud perpetrator will locate a property which may be valued at a normal market price. This person has been known to hire a dishonest appraiser and have that appraiser appraise the property for two or three times its actual value or any value exceeding the property's real value. The fraud perpetrator, using the straw buyer's information and credit rating, will obtain financing for the straw buyer through a mortgage company. This is usually 100 percent financing and all the straw buyer has to do is appear at the closing attorney's office for the closing. As most people know, real estate closings involve a tremendous amount of paperwork to be signed. The straw buyer usually doesn't read any of the documents because they trust the fraud perpetrator to have arranged everything for them. During the closing and some imaginative maneuvers on the part of the fraud perpetrator, checks are disbursed or wire transfers made. Of course the seller will receive a check or wire transfer for the sale of his or her property, fees will be subtracted, and the fraud perpetrator will receive a check or wire transfer into his or her account. The fraud perpetrator will either have some type of mechanical lien on the property or the note contains remodeling expenses which have yet to be done. The latter usually involves the appraiser taking into consideration these improvements and then issuing the appraisal based on those improvements. The fraud perpetrator receives his or her proceeds from the sale but never had any intention of doing any work whatsoever. The suspect(s) will attempt to have the straw buyer purchase as many properties as possible in this manner in the allowable time.

After three or four months pass, the straw buyer becomes aware that something is terribly wrong. They now own several properties and are in debt between $500,000 and $1,000,000. They have not seen or heard from the fraud perpetrator and the fraud perpetrator did not find any renters for the properties. The straw buyer is now faced owing several months of past due mortgage payments which they cannot possibly pay. As the straw buyer begins to realize, they now own several properties that are worth about a third to a half of what they had paid. I discovered that most straw buyers have one thing in common. Whenever asked if they had seen the property before they purchased it, they always replied "no". Most straw buyers rely on the fraud perpetrators to handle everything so they take the word of the perpetrator that the property is worth the amount of the purchase. The suspect will usually double and sometimes triple his or her initial investment leaving the person who purchased the property with a property that is actually worth about one third or one half of its true value. The buyer of the property will sometimes be able to make the payments on the property but most buyers cannot. The property will then enter into foreclosure and, in the process, place the buyer in financial ruin.

Since this variation of mortgage fraud can be detected by honest and knowledgeable individuals, the mortgage fraud perpetrator's second option is to become the owner of the property and then quickly resell the property to a straw buyer or unsuspecting buyer. This is known as flipping the property. Flipping is perfectly legal in every state as long as everything is done by the numbers and legally. A lot of people have made a lot of money, even to the extent of becoming millionaires, by flipping houses. People will often purchase a property, a fixer upper, and then make any necessary repairs or perhaps even remodel the residence. After investing in the repairs or the remodel, the person resells the property to someone else for a profit. This is perfectly legal. When does it become illegal? Mortgage fraud occurs anytime deceit lies, and/or dishonesty is used by any member of the transaction. For instance, a person purchases a residence for, let's say $90,000. He or she then spends another $25,000 in repairs and remodeling to the house. The house is then appraised for $150,000. The owner sells the property for that amount and walks away with $35,000 profit minus some other fees and expenses. The sale is legitimate as long as the property is worth $150,000. If the property had only been worth $115,000 after the repairs but the appraised value was fraudulently obtained to reflect a falsified price of $150,000, then you have fraud.

Often, the fraud perpetrator will fabricate the straw buyer's income with false statements and counterfeit pay stubs. This enables the buyer to purchase a piece of real estate which they might not be able to afford otherwise. The fraud perpetrator will also usually list the residence as the buyers' principal residence and not that of an investment. Another common method of the fraud perpetrator is to obtain financing for the straw buyer for two or three houses within an extremely short time period. By doing this, the fraud perpetrator is able to receive illegal proceeds on two or more transactions without a lender discovering the real truth. If a lender discovers that the buyer has another or perhaps two more properties under contract, the lender will probably not approve the loan.

One problem fraud detectives will encounter when investigating a mortgage fraud is attempting to differentiate between the fraud perpetrator or perpetrators and those that were just caught up in the illegal act. Appraisers can often be caught up in the scam. These individuals receive specialized training to be able to advise someone what a particular property is worth.

Appraisers use several methods to appraise a property and one in particular is the use of comparables. This method requires the appraiser to locate similar houses or structures within close proximity of the house or structure being appraised. It also requires researching real estate documents for recent sales of those comparables. This can create a big problem with the appraisal if the community has been subjected to a lot of previous mortgage fraud. This can lead the appraiser to unknowingly give an inaccurate appraisal of the subject property because other comparables have sold for amounts greatly exaggerated. Before an appraiser can be charged, a fraud detective must be able to prove that the appraiser took an active part in the fraud and that they, knowingly, used deception in their appraisal of the subject property and not through incompetence or mistake.

There are many scenarios for a mortgage fraud; however, it usually involves someone receiving funds for a particular property which the actual value has been exaggerated. One such mortgage fraud investigation involved a husband and wife team. This investigation began when an attorney and manager for an investment bank came to the fraud office to speak with me about an employee theft. The employee had been hired as a financial advisor for the firm and the manager of the firm had discovered that an employee had stolen over a half of a million dollars in funds belonging to a client and the company.

As we began to investigate the case, it was discovered that the financial advisor had used the stolen identity of the victim to also purchase an expensive residence just south of Atlanta in an exclusive sub-division. The victim was unaware of the transaction which the suspects kept hidden. The suspects were living in the residence and eventually fabricated paperwork which enabled them to purchase the house from the unsuspecting and unaware victim. As the investigation continued, it was discovered that the two suspects had an extensive knowledge of the real estate business because the female was listed as an agent and the male was employed as a broker. Our investigation discovered that they had set up and incorporated a bogus mortgage business. They used what is referred to as a virtual office to conduct much of their illegal business. A virtual office is an office that is rented and usually has a prestigious address. The virtual office allows the renter to give the impression that the business is located at the prestigious address in the city. It also provides the business with an answering or messaging center and the use of the conference room, if desired. Through a series of premeditated and ingenious moves, they were able to purchase houses and have funds diverted into the accounts of the fake business.

The investigation uncovered several properties that the two suspects had purchased using this method. In reality, the two were running an underground mortgage company to acquire and sell real estate. As I was investigating these suspects, I came across an earlier suspected mortgage fraud involving the two suspects in another state. This incident, occurred over fifteen years earlier and, involved the purchase of a particular piece of property. The purchase price of that property, at that particular time, was $115,000. The suspect refinanced the property two years later for a higher amount and then again two years after that for still even another higher amount. Then in 1996, on the same day, the suspects did three things. First, they refinanced the property at again a higher amount. Second, the suspect added another person to the deed. This I have yet to understand. And third, the suspect changed the deed over to an attorney. Three months after this, the residence went in to foreclosure. Normally, mortgage fraud will end with the foreclosure of a residence and the mortgage company or lender will be left holding the bag. This particular incident wasn't over just yet though; the residence, after being foreclosed, was placed up for auction on the court house steps. The auction was conducted and the house was sold for $210,000. The winning bidder was the husband of the suspect. That winning bid was then transferred to the nephew of the suspect and he obtained a loan of $289,000 for the property. By 1998, two years after being sold on the court house steps, the property was once again in foreclosure.

Another method of a mortgage fraud perpetrator is for the fraud perpetrator to actually appear to be someone else. This is done using a stolen identity. Often, the fraud perpetrator will hire someone to use the victim's identity and provide him with a counterfeit identification card so that he can attend the closing. Several months after the transaction has been completed, the victim of the stolen identity will be contacted by a mortgage company advising him or her that they are several months behind on their mortgage payment. That is when they discover that they now own a property in some other city and state. This method can be used by the owner/seller of the subject property to obtain the maximum amount of profit from the sale and provide for an immediate sell. It can also be accomplished by anyone standing to gain a profit from the sale. The bottom line is a property is usually sold very fast and the fraud perpetrators receive their funds.

Yet, still another method of mortgage fraud involves the filing of a quit claim deed in the county court house by the fraud perpetrator. In most of these cases, the fraud perpetrator will research properties until they find the property that can be used for the crime. These properties usually involve an absentee owner. The true owner of the property obtained ownership either as being an heir to the original owner or had purchased the property and is now renting the property or keeping the property as an investment property. These properties are completely paid for and do not contain any liens. The suspect will enter the court house and file a fraudulent quit claim deed on the property containing the forged signature of the victim. Sometimes, the victim will discover this early before the fraud perpetrator can accomplish what he/she was attempting. The victim needs to file an affidavit of fraud and forgery with the court house and have it placed on record. The victim will probably encounter many obstacles in their quest to have the fraudulent quit claim deed removed from the file. This definitely needs to be changed. If a public document is fraudulent in nature and that document was originated with the intent to deceive and/or defraud the true owner of the property, it has no place in a public file.

Serious situations can and have developed when a fraud perpetrator uses or used a quit claim deed on a property. The fraud suspect, after filing the fraudulent quit claim deed, will then either refinance the property or sell the property to a second victim. Now you have two victims or possibly three if you take in to account the loan company. Needless to say, victims faced with this situation feel an enormous amount of stress and anxiety. They will also incur an enormous amount of legal fees attempting to decide who the rightful owner is. In most cases, the rightful owner is the original owner. The secondary victim and his/her loan company will more than likely be at a loss.

Mortgage fraud perpetrators have the capability of stealing a large amount of currency. Who pays for the loss that is incurred? We do and citizens of each and every community do. After a mortgage fraud perpetrator has done his or her dirty deed, the subject property usually gets foreclosed. During this time, other perpetrators will use the property to sell drugs and use the property for prostitution. The neighborhood that was once safe for you and your family is no longer safe. Whenever and wherever mortgage fraud exists, the community will pay for it through higher taxes and a dramatic climb in criminal activity. It is a crime that can affect a lot of people, today and tomorrow.

Chapter Sixteen

The Drug Nexus

A major connection exists between the world of fraud and the world of illegal drugs. In our modern era, the two coincide more often than not. Many fraud perpetrators use illegal drugs and some will commit fraudulent criminal acts to help facilitate their illegal drug or narcotic activities.

The Atlanta Police Department's Major Fraud Unit has investigated many groups that were deeply into fraud and identity theft but also had a drug connection. Drugs of choice are marijuana, cocaine and its derivatives, heroin, and methamphetamine or crystal meth. Crystal meth is perhaps one of the most addictive illegal drugs available and it is commonly found in both rural areas and large cities. In recent years, it has become such a large problem that many states now require stores that sell antihistamine products to limit the number of sales, register the purchaser's name and address, and to have these products behind the counter or in a locked display. The fraud perpetrator who is hooked on crystal meth is referred to as a "Geek monster". These individuals have been known to stay on a high for several days without any sleep. When the high finally leaves, they will normally sleep for long periods of time. But it is while they are on the high that they do the most damage. During this time they plan and execute their illegal fraudulent schemes.

A few years back, we came across a semi organized group of people committing similar types of fraud. Before it was all said and done, we identified approximately 40 people associated with this particular group and made more than 32 arrests. The group started to reveal itself when several of its members began to be arrested on fraud related crimes. I had been working several cases prior to this group being identified but only began to identify several members after the arrest of their associates. We eventually were able to identify and arrest the suspects responsible for the crimes.

The first significant arrest came at a four star hotel in the Buckhead area of Atlanta. A patrol officer working his beat had responded to the hotel on a possible credit card fraud. Prior to his arrival at the location, hotel security had pulled two individuals from a rented hotel room and was attempting to interview the two people about the suspicious credit card account number. As they were relocating to the hotel's office area, one of the suspects broke away and ran out of the hotel. When the officer arrived at the hotel, hotel security advised him that one of the suspects had run away. The officer was able to obtain a description of the suspect that ran away and placed a radio call to other units in the area. An off duty officer heard the B.O.L.O. and spotted the suspect walking on the sidewalk a few blocks from the hotel. The off duty officer reported that the suspect was carrying two bags and he was attempting to stop the suspect. When the suspect saw the officer, he attempted to run away again. The off duty officer chased the suspect into a parking area and observed the suspect throw the two carry bags underneath a parked car. After a short foot pursuit, the officer was able to apprehend the suspect. The officer was also able to recover the two bags which the suspect had thrown underneath the parked vehicle.

The suspect and his bags were returned to the hotel. Hotel security positively identified the suspect as the person who had rented the room and the person who had ran away. The responding officer located several counterfeit checks, credit card numbers, and counterfeit identification cards on the latter suspect's personal effects. The officer requested that I come to the scene and conduct an investigation. Upon my arrival at the hotel, I met with the hotel's manager concerning the credit card number which had been used to book the room. The manager stated that the charge had not been approved and believed that the credit card number could possibly be stolen. The suspect who had run away from the officer was already under arrest for obstruction and the other suspect was being detained. I advised each of their Constitution Rights. The suspect being detained was eager to talk; however, the second suspect who was under arrest was not. The second suspect even went as far as saying to the first suspect "You've got the right to remain silent, use it. Shut the fuck up." The suspect being detained stated that he had met the second suspect the previous day and that the second suspect told him that he had a rented hotel room in a very nice hotel and the two of them could party. The suspect went on to say that he had nothing to do with renting the hotel room and did not know whose credit card number had been used to rent the hotel room.

I contacted the credit card company attempting to ascertain if the card number in question had been stolen. The credit card company's representative was attempting to verify with the card holder. The two suspects were taken to the Major Fraud office for processing. Within the two carry bags that the second suspect had discarded, we discovered stolen mail, stolen receipts, credit card numbers, and counterfeit checks. One suspect was booked on misdemeanor charges for not being able to pay the hotel room and the second suspect who was originally arrested for obstruction, now had several felony charges for fraud related crimes. This suspect still refused to talk to me but did begin to cry when I informed him of his charges. He asked if he could call his mother in Florida and I told him that he could. I dialed the number for him and let him explain his circumstances to his mother and I advised him of the jail's location. The two suspects were then taken to the Fulton County Detention Center.

After the two suspects were taken to the Fulton County Jail, the hotel's security director telephoned me and told me that the two suspects had a parked vehicle in the hotel's parking deck and that the vehicle appeared full of boxes and suitcases. Detective Cooper and I drove to the location and inspected the vehicle. As the hotel's security director had described, it was full of items and boxes. Upon our return to the Major Fraud office, I drafted a search warrant and affidavit for the suspect's vehicle and took it to Superior Court to have a Superior Court Judge sign off on it. After obtaining a Superior Court Judge's signature, we drove back to the parking area and impounded the vehicle. The vehicle was then searched for further evidence. We discovered several boxes of stolen information which had been stolen from the records section of an area rental agency. We also discovered a small scale and a large number of small plastic bags. As we found these items, we requested a K-9 Unit respond to the scene. The K-9 hit on the lining of a black suitcase which had been in the trunk area of the vehicle. Upon closer inspection of the suitcase's liner, it was discovered that the liner could be pulled back. As we pulled the liner back, a small white bag of suspected methamphetamine, crystal meth, or ice fell out to the ground. After these discoveries, we returned to the Major Fraud office and drew up more warrants for the charges involving the stolen records and for the illegal drugs.

Almost a month passed before we had another related arrest to the case. It was pretty much the same scenario, only this time it was at a different four star hotel in the Buckhead area. The hotel's security director had notified the Atlanta Police after being notified that two guests staying in one of the hotel's rooms had used a stolen credit card number to rent the hotel room. The security director had confirmed the credit card number as stolen through the credit card company and then contacted the Atlanta Police. The same officer working his beat was dispatched to the location. The officer and the security director went to the hotel room of the two suspects and made entry into the hotel room detaining one person. The officer requested assistance and a sergeant from the Buckhead precinct responded to the location. As the sergeant and the officer obtained information regarding the stolen credit card number, the sergeant called for assistance from the Major Fraud Unit. I responded to the location and walked inside of the hotel room joining the sergeant, officer, and security director. Laying about the room were several checks which I automatically recognized as being counterfeit and were of the same stock and style as the counterfeit checks recovered from the first suspect. To make matters worse for the suspect, a large amount of crystal methamphetamine was discovered in the hotel room.

I advised the suspect of his Constitutional Rights and he agreed to speak with me without an attorney being present. The suspect wanted to cut a deal and said that he would give up other players in the gang to obtain his freedom. I told him that I could not make the deal but I would go to bat for him and speak on his behalf if he became a cooperating defendant. The suspect was reluctant, at first, but agreed to give me information. As the officer was transporting the suspect to the county jail, I told him that I would be over to speak with him the following morning.

The next morning, we interviewed the suspect. This was not your ordinary suspect. He was very well educated with degrees in English and business. As I began the interview, I began to ask him questions about his life and career and how he got caught up in all of this mess. He said that after college, he worked and then eventually started his own business. Then one night, several years ago, he went to a local strip club with a few of his friends. While at the club, he met a dancer. He and the dancer became romantically involved and he would visit the club regularly. The dancer and her friends introduced him to crystal methamphetamine. Within a short period of time, all of his money was gone and his business was in ruins. The suspect said that he and the dancer had a child together but that they had recently broken up and he had not seen the child in some time. The suspect said that he had been introduced to several members of this drug ring who were committing fraud to facilitate their crystal methamphetamine habit and he told me that he had started hanging around these other members more and more.

The suspect told us that the members of the gang would check into hotels and then late at night, when the hotel staff was at its minimum, would steal hotel documents which contained the personal information of hotel guests both present and past and also information regarding business accounts. He told us that hotels usually kept old records in hall storage closets which were often left unlocked. At other times, he said that one fraud perpetrator would distract the night clerk while the other fraud perpetrator(s) raided the books. Hotel records often reflect everything a fraud perpetrator needs to steal a person's identity. We have recovered stolen hotel records with the victim's name and address, credit card information, and a copy of their driver's license. With this, the fraud perpetrator can become you using your credit card number and if questions arise about your identity, they can fall back on the copy of the driver's license even obtaining a counterfeit identification card with your information with the suspect's picture.

This group would often telephone or fax an Atlanta hotel claiming to be a representative of a business using one of the stolen compromised credit card numbers from one of their thefts. The so-called representative would book several nights stays at the hotel for either him or a guest. Much of the time, this process worked since most of the victims did not know that their credit card number had been compromised. In a few cases, credit card companies became suspicious of the charges and called the credit card holder. After speaking with the victim and confirming that the charges were not valid, the credit card company would then contact the hotel and the hotel, in turn, would contact the Atlanta Police Department.

The cooperating defendant told us a lot of what we did not know. We began to identify several individuals within the gang and began to arrest them for various fraud related crimes. These suspects, for the most part, were not everyday street criminals. They were mostly from middle class working families who had gone astray because of crystal methamphetamine. Just about all of the individuals we arrested cooperated with the investigation leading us to identify and eventually arrest many others.

Most people hooked on crystal methamphetamine do not work regular jobs. Therefore, to live, eat, and party they must find another way. Since most of these kids have broken off from their families, they rely on stealing, prostitution, and fraud to support their lifestyles. We discovered that many of these suspects would rent a vehicle from a car rental agency using a stolen credit card number. After obtaining the vehicle, they would drive it awhile and then trade it off for a substantial amount of crystal methamphetamine. The car rental agency would, after a month or so, report the vehicle as being stolen. These cars would eventually be recovered but only after changing hands several times. At first, we thought that the rented hotel rooms were used by the members of this gang as somewhere nice to party but it became evident that the majority of this gang was homeless much of the time. Jumping hotel room to hotel room was one way to keep warm and dry. Crystal methamphetamine suspects rarely keep a regular place to live because all of their funds are used to support their drug habit. The suspects would sometimes place an online order for electronics such as laptop computers, cellular telephones, and televisions using the stolen credit card numbers and have the items shipped to one of the area hotels. The suspect or a friend of the suspect would then retrieve the item or items from the hotel. After obtaining these items, the suspects would then sale the items or trade them off for a certain amount of crystal methamphetamine.

We were able to identify two of main players of this organization and eventually arrest both. One of these would often recruit others and teach them how to commit fraud. He was well versed at counterfeit checks, identity fraud, and credit card fraud. I had been attempting to identify him for several months but was unable to do so until we arrested several people in this operation. This particular suspect committed a tremendous amount of fraudulent criminal acts. I first became aware of his fraudulent counterfeit checks when he used the compromised checking accounts of a large real estate development firm to purchase laptops from electronic stores around Atlanta and in Phoenix, Arizona. At the same time, a detective from the Alpharetta Police Department was also investigating a case of severe identity fraud in which the suspect had used a stolen identity to purchase a new vehicle and charge thousands of dollars on stolen credit cards. The suspect was one and the same. Through our investigation, it was discovered that the suspect was also dealing in crystal methamphetamine and would make trips to Arizona to purchase the drug.

It took several months for the suspect to be apprehended. An alert employee of an electronic store, in a jurisdiction west of Atlanta, became suspicious of the person attempting to purchase several laptop computers and notified the local agency. As officers responded to the scene, the suspect attempted to flee but officers were able to pursue him. After a brief car chase, the suspect was apprehended in the stolen vehicle. Inside of the vehicle, he possessed more than 100 personal identifiers of unaware victims. He also had a large amount of crystal methamphetamine on his person. The suspect was given a sentence of ten years but was released on probation only after serving about six months in jail. After getting out of jail, the suspect returned to his old fraud habits and crystal methamphetamine use. He had leased an apartment, in the Buckhead area of Atlanta, using the stolen identifiers of a person and had set up shop committing the same types of crimes he had done before. After my retirement, I learned that arrest warrants for the suspect had been obtained and he was arrested once again.

Chapter Seventeen

Nigerian Fraud

I have had several investigations, in my career, involving individuals of Nigerian decent. A lot of the fraud reports that have been made can be attributed to Nigerians or from people who have copied their fraud activities and scams.

Task forces have been developed over the years by federal, state, and local agencies to combat Nigerian fraud. Please take note, not everyone who is of Nigerian decent is a criminal or fraud perpetrator. Task forces were developed because of the large number of crimes, such as the 4-1-9 letter, being committed by a large number of people who were Nigerian. People can often group people as a certain kind; however, as the old saying goes one bad apple does not ruin the whole bunch. I know that the Nigerian government and its hard working people do not want that association and who could blame them. The real culprits are those who have committed the fraudulent crimes and who continue to do so.

I hope everyone is aware of the 4-1-9 advanced fee scam or Nigerian letters. I know several prominent business men in Atlanta have received such letters and immediately notified the fraud unit. If you are not aware of such things, they typically go like this. You receive a letter or an email from someone saying that they are from an African nation that has or is going through a civil war. The letter states that the sender was at one time a very wealthy person or his or her family was very wealthy. But do to the change in government; all of their assets have been frozen. To unfreeze these assets, the sender requests that you submit funds to help cover the cost of attorney's fees, taxes, etc. The amount of fees requested varies with each particular letter. In return for your funds, you are promised a percentage of the sender's or sender's family assets. A lot of people throughout the years have been victimized by these fraud perpetrators and have lost a lot of money. Perpetrators will use this particular scam in various ways. They have been known to tell their victims that they were from a South African country and lately, perpetrators have been using Middle Eastern countries as the place of their former residence. These perpetrators will make every attempt to make their scheme believable. As always, potential victims should be on their guard. Remember, if something sounds too good to be true it probably isn't true. The majority of times, good things require a lot of hard work and time to receive any reward.

Another scheme of these perpetrators often involves sending the victim a letter accompanied with a counterfeit check. The letter explains that the victim has just won or is a partial winner to the Canadian Lottery, European Lottery, or some other type of lottery. The victim often falls for this scheme even though he or she never entered such a lottery. The victim is instructed to cash the counterfeit check or deposit the counterfeit check into their checking account and then remit the proceeds through a wire transfer. The victims are told that this will cover the costs of any processing fees and any other fees or taxes. After submitting the funds through a wire transfer, the victims are told that the proceeds from their lottery winnings will be sent to them. Now guess what? First, they were never actually winners to begin with. Second, the check deposited into their checking account or that they had cashed is 100 percent counterfeit. The victim never receives any lottery winnings and to make matters worse could face felony criminal charges and have to repay the funds to their banking institution or check cashing agency.

Several years ago, a security guard walking the parking area of a local high rise business complex came across a vehicle parked in the parking area. The security guard noticed that inside of the parked vehicle, were several large containers containing some type of liquid, boxes, gloves, and other items. The guard's first instinct told him that this was a bomb or perhaps bomb materials. He immediately notified 911, officers and S.W.A.T. responded to the scene. The area was evacuated and S.W.A.T. opened the vehicle and checked the interior's contents. After clearing the scene and finding that the vehicle did not contain a bomb or any bomb materials, S.W.A.T. notified the Major Fraud Unit to respond. Inside of the vehicle were materials used by several Nigerian fraud perpetrators in the Black Money Scam.

The perpetrators will convince someone that they are smuggling in large amounts of currency which had been hidden and kept out of the hands of the government, stolen currency which has been smuggled, or perhaps, drug money that has been smuggled into the country. The perpetrators tell the willing victim that the currency has been dyed and special chemicals are needed to revive the currency to its original state. The victim is shown a trey supposedly containing the special chemicals. The perpetrators then show the victim a dyed bill or perhaps a couple of dyed bills and explain that once dipped in the special chemicals, the bills will look new again. The suspects then use a sleight of hand trick as they drop the dyed bill(s) in the solution and then retrieve different bills from the bottom of the tank or tray. The victim is amazed as the currency comes out of the solution clean of any dyes. The victims are told that for an amount that they can purchase the chemicals needed to clean the bills and in return they will receive a large portion of the cleaned bills. The victims actually believe that they are going to make 100%, 200%, or better return on their money. This particular scam requires, at least, one fraud suspect meet the victim face to face and the fraud perpetrator(s) know that his or her chance of being detected and arrested for the fraudulent crime is much greater than most of their other scams or cons. After the fraud perpetrator(s) receive the victim's funds, the fraud perpetrator(s) will do one of two things, he or she might attempt to convince the victim that more funds are needed to obtain the chemicals and dyed bills because some type of problem has arisen or the suspect(s) will exit the meeting and the victim will never see or hear from them again.

A favorite scam, of several Nigerian fraud perpetrators, is to attempt to purchase a vehicle or any other item which is for sale. This scam runs something like this. The fraud perpetrator will locate an item which someone has for sale. This item, usually a vehicle, is being sold by an individual through a newspaper, magazine, or through online advertisements. In one particular case, the victim ran an advertisement through an online service. The victim was selling his late model vehicle for $13,000.00. After placing the advertisement, the victim began receiving emails from the suspect inquiring about the vehicle. After a couple of emails had been exchanged, the suspect agreed to purchase the vehicle for the asking price of $13,000.00. The suspect told the victim that he would receive a check the following day, by overnight mail, and the suspect would arrange for someone to pick up the vehicle within a few days. Later on that day, the suspect emailed the victim advising him that his secretary had made a mistake and that she had mailed him the wrong check. The check was made payable to the victim however the suspect told the victim that his secretary had sent the wrong amount. He said that the check had been made out for $20,000.00 which was to have gone to someone else and that the other person had gotten a check in the amount of $13,000.00. The suspect told the victim that he trusted him and that for him to go ahead and cash the $20,000 check, keep $13,000, and then wire transfer the remaining $7,000 back to the suspect. The unsuspecting victim attempted to do just that. He went down to the local check cashing agency and presented the check to be cashed. The cashier at the check cashing agency notified 911 upon the discovery that the check was counterfeit. The victim was still standing in the lobby, waiting, when the Atlanta Police Officer arrived. It was fortunate that this call was handled by a veteran officer who knew fraud. The officer immediately realized that the victim was not a perpetrator. The veteran officer notified me and then brought the victim to my office.

Once in my office, the victim began to tell me everything that had occurred and was able to show me the advertisement and the emails he had received from the suspect. The victim had no previous arrests and he was a student working on his degree. If the responding officer had been inexperienced, this victim could had been arrested for forgery in the first degree and taken to jail. He might not have been convicted but who wants to take that chance. After interviewing the victim and reviewing the documents, I had the victim email the suspect telling him that he had cashed the check but would not wire the $7,000 because he felt it unsafe. I had the victim tell the suspect that he would only hand over the $7,000 to someone in person. I was trying to pull the suspect in and exact an arrest on him. The suspect sent numerous emails to the victim eventually telling him that he was hiring a Columbian hit man to kill him. The victim became nervous and scared. I had the victim send one last email to the perpetrator which included my information and that the suspect was to contact me immediately. The emails and the threats ceased after that. In retrospect, I guess that I shouldn't have involved the victim, in an attempt, to make an apprehension.

Several years back, I was working an uniformed car in the business district of Atlanta. I was a liaison of the Atlanta Police Department and the business district. I began to receive numerous complaints from victims and security directors about luxury vehicles being stolen from their parking decks. It seemed that about every other day or so, I was taking a police report on a stolen luxury vehicle. Within a short period of time, I had a lot of luxury cars stolen off of my beat. The security directors all got together and put together a task force which included the building security directors, officers/detectives from surrounding police agencies, and federal agents. Only a couple of the buildings had any video surveillance equipment and the visual information obtained did not reveal a lot of suspect information. Another fact was that there wasn't any broken glass in the area of the stolen vehicles and no witnesses to any of the incidents could be located.

One victim who had his brand new $75,000 vehicle stolen from a gated parking deck called me the following day and said that someone had ordered a spare key to his vehicle from a local dealer a few weeks before the theft. A second victim had his pride and joy parked in the parking deck. He, too, discovered the vehicle stolen as he had left his office. This vehicle was recovered the following day. The suspect had driven the car to another location and had left the vehicle there as he test drove another similar luxury vehicle. The owner of the latter vehicle became suspicious after several hours had passed and the suspect had not returned. When he notified the police department, it was discovered that the vehicle the suspect had left, for collateral, was reported stolen. I don't believe that the owner of the second vehicle ever recovered his car. The victim, whose vehicle was used as collateral, was able to recover his stolen vehicle without any damage; however, the perpetrators were not through with him. About a week later, the same victim called to make another report regarding his vehicle being stolen. Once again, it was recovered and had been used, as collateral, while the suspect stole another car.

It became evident that we were dealing with an organized car theft ring and that they had a shopping list of makes and models. It took awhile but our auto theft unit was able to get the assistance of several local dealerships. One of the suspects had entered the dealership and had placed an order for a set of keys telling the dealership that he had just purchased the vehicle and needed the keys as soon as possible. The dealership notified our auto theft unit and when the suspect arrived to pick up the keys, our auto theft detectives were acting as the employees of the dealership. The suspect was apprehended and was found to be driving a stolen vehicle. Our auto theft unit did a tremendous job on this one. They had numerous felony charges on this suspect for stealing several cars. The lead detective, in the case, would execute a warrant for a particular vehicle for the suspect's arrest each and every time he posted bond. After awhile, the suspect at the request of his attorney began to cooperate. This arrest lead to several more arrests, the recovery of several stolen vehicles, and the discovery of the fraudulent operation.

The originators of this car theft ring were Nigerian. They had figured out that by obtaining the vehicle identification number of the vehicle and the tag number, they could then fabricate counterfeit registration cards for the vehicle. The suspects would drive around the business district of Atlanta searching for a particular luxury vehicle make and model. Once they found this vehicle, they would tail the driver either to his or her office complex or residence. Once the vehicle was parked, the suspects would obtain the V.I.N. and tag number by using a small digital camera, camera phone, or by simply writing it down on a piece of paper. After doing this, they were able to produce a counterfeit registration card on their personal computer and printer. The suspects then recruited another suspect who entered a dealership armed with a counterfeit identification card and the counterfeit registration card. The suspect would then tell the dealership that he had just purchased the vehicle and needed a new set of keys for his car. The suspects always paid in cash and always placed a rush order.

The suspects knew that most luxury vehicles are equipped with keys containing an electronic or computer chip. Keys of this type are made at the manufacturer and usually stored at the manufacturer's storage facility. Once the suspects obtained the key for the vehicle, they knew exactly where to locate the vehicle again. When they did, the vehicle was stolen. It was discovered through investigation that after stealing the vehicles, the perpetrators changed the vehicle identification numbers on several of the vehicles with the exception of one area. Most of the vehicles were then shipped to Nigeria. A couple of vehicles were located at a couple of dealerships after someone discovered the vehicle had two different identification numbers on it.

A couple of years ago, Special Agents with the Federal Bureau of Investigation and detectives with the Atlanta Police Department's Fugitive Unit were executing an arrest warrant on a Nigerian in the Buckhead area of Atlanta. The Nigerian had come to the United States during the late eighties and had started doing fraud. He was arrested, convicted, and served time in prison for his crimes. After being released, he was deported back to Nigeria. Within two years after being deported, he was back in the United States under an assumed name. He met and married a lady and together they had a daughter. However, the relationship did not last long and the couple filed for divorce. The suspect's ex-wife was granted custody of their daughter and the suspect received visitation rights. During one such visitation period, the suspect took his daughter to Nigeria to visit his relatives. Upon his return to the United States, he left his daughter with his relatives to be raised and attend school. The mother of the child went through several agencies and a long, trying time trying to regain her child. The suspect was ordered to bring the child back to the United States and to the child's mother. The suspect ignored this order and refused to cooperate. A warrant was obtained for his arrest. To avoid arrest, the suspect moved to Atlanta.

Special Agents and detectives located the suspect at an apartment complex and executed the arrest warrant. While executing the arrest, inside of the suspect's apartment, the agents and detectives noticed a large amount of U.S. currency, in plain view, on his kitchen counter and also a large number of personal identifiers such as names, dates of births, social security numbers, etc. laying about the apartment. They recognized this to be evidence of identity theft and called the fraud unit in to investigate.

Detective Cooper obtained a search warrant for the apartment based on what the special agents and detectives had witnessed in plain view. The search warrant was granted and inside of the apartment we discovered more evidence of identity fraud. The suspect had used the stolen personal information of numerous victims to obtain eloans, credit cards, and vehicle loans which he used to purchase used luxury vehicles. The suspect had a shopping list of used vehicles written on a pad and had marked several listed vehicles in auto trading magazines. The suspect would pretend to be someone else by stealing their identity and apply for a car loan on line using the victim's personal information. When he received the check, he would purchase the vehicle. Shortly thereafter, he would resell the vehicle for cash. The victim and the loan company would not know that they had been victimized for several months. Inside this suspect's apartment were leather furniture, flat screen televisions, computers, and printers. We discovered a closet full of designer suits, dress clothes, and shoes. We also discovered numerous tune-up and repair bills exceeding $10,000 for his late model luxury vehicle which was parked in the parking lot. The icing on the cake, so to speak, was when we found his tax return for the previous year. He had filed an annual earnings statement of $13,000 as a taxi driver.

You would think that this case was about to come to a conclusion. A couple of months after his arrest the suspect supplied the United States Postal Service Inspector, assigned to the case, with evidence of another Nigerian suspect living in the same complex committing identity fraud. Armed with this and evidence directly related to the second Nigerian fraud perpetrator, we obtained another search warrant for a different apartment in the same complex. Once inside, we found still more evidence of identity fraud and stolen items. The second suspect was arrested and I advised him of his Constitutional Rights. He said that he understood these Rights and agreed to speak with me without an attorney. As I began questioning him concerning the identity thefts, I began to notice the furniture in the apartment. It appeared to be the same exact furniture from the first suspect's apartment. I asked him if the furniture was the same furniture and he replied "yes". He said that after the first suspect had been arrested he had gone into the apartment and had moved it all into his apartment. When I asked him if the furniture had been stolen, he replied "Yes, it had all been bought using stolen information."

People can prevent becoming victims of such scams as the advance money scam, black money scam, and lottery scam. The very first thing for the victim to remember that if it sounds too good to be true, then it probably isn't true. Numerous victims have been taken because they become greedy and let their greed get in the way of good judgment. Many victims think that they can make a tremendous return on their investment without any work and in a very short time. A good rule of thumb to follow is that good things take time and nothing can be accomplished without a lot of hard work. As far as the lottery scam goes, you cannot, and I repeat cannot, win something that you did not play. On a special note, if you are thinking of participating in some type of foreign lottery, I would highly recommend checking with authorities first because it may be illegal. If a perfect stranger sends you a check, always investigate first. Take the check to your local bank or call the banking institution that the check is drawn on to find out if the check is legitimate. When contacting the banking institution that the check was drawn on, make sure that you do not call the telephone number which may be imprinted on the check. Always check the phone number through the yellow pages or some other telephone number locator. Under no circumstances, deposit the check into your account or attempt to cash the check without first investigating and verifying. If you do discover it is fraudulent, notify your local police department and describe the incident in full.

Chapter Eighteen

The Pigeon Drop

A few scams have lasted several decades and even though most people have heard of these scams before they still produce quite a number of victims each and every year. Such a scam is the pigeon drop. Most people think of a pigeon as mainly a species of birds but it may be used to describe people who are easily swindled out of their money.

Every so often, we had cases such as the pigeon drop. I will describe a couple with the hope that innocent victims will be alerted when one of these con men or con women approach them. If ever approached with one of the following, run away from the perpetrators as quickly as possible and get far away from them. Immediately alert others, law enforcement, and the media, of the suspect's intentions and scam.

One variation of the pigeon drop scam occurred at mall in Atlanta. The victim had just left the grocery store and had gotten into her vehicle parked in the parking area. As she was starting the car, the female suspect approached the car and gently tapped on the driver's side window. The victim rolled the window down to find out what the person wanted. The suspect then asked if the victim had dropped a bank bag. The female suspect then bent over and picked up the bank bag revealing it to the victim. Of course, the victim said no, it was not hers. The female suspect opened the bank bag slightly. Inside of the bank bag appeared to be a lot of money. The female suspect then told the victim that it was probably drug money or money from some type of illegal activity and must have fallen from someone's vehicle. The female suspect immediately closed the bank bag and told the victim that it was now found property. The female suspect told the victim that she knew of an attorney that could help them and together they could split the money and receive the proceeds legally. The victim agreed. The suspect then got into the victim's vehicle and proceeded to give her directions to the attorney's office.

As the victim drove the suspect to a business complex, the suspect began conversing with the victim. The suspect told the victim that they would probably have to pay taxes on the found currency. The victim told the suspect that she didn't have a lot of savings, just a little over $5,000 in her account and hoped that would be enough. That is exactly what the suspect was looking for. The victim or mark had just given the fraud suspect the amount which she would then target. When they arrived at the complex, the suspect got out of the vehicle with the found bank bag and entered the business complex while the victim parked her car. About fifteen to twenty minutes later, the suspect returned to the victim's vehicle without the bank bag. The suspect told the victim that the bank bag contained over $10,000 in currency and that the attorney's office had cut them a cashier's check in that amount and had used the rest of the currency to pay the taxes and fees. The suspect convinced the victim that because she did not have any identification, she could not cash the check. The suspect was able to get the victim to go to her bank and withdraw $5000 from her account. In exchange for the $5000 in currency, the suspect gave the victim the $10,000 check. The suspect then told the victim that she had a previous engagement and had the victim drop her off at a nearby street corner.

The victim soon discovered that the $10,000 cashier's check was counterfeit. In addition, she also discovered that no attorney was listed at the business complex. She was now out $5,000, which was just about all the money in the world she had. She could not make her house payment that month and I know she suffered a great deal. Once again, the fraud perpetrator was able to pull off such a clever scam because the victim dropped her guard.

This case, compares to the case in the previous paragraph; however, the loss in this case greatly exceeded the loss of the previous one. The suspects, in this case, researched their target, the victim, before ever approaching her. The victim, an elderly lady, had just left a store in a busy complex, walked to her vehicle, and got inside. As she was about to start the vehicle, the female suspect gently tapped on her window. As the victim rolled her window down, the female suspect asked her if she had dropped a bank bag. The victim told the suspect no. The suspect then unzipped the bank bag and pulled out a couple of hundred dollar bills. The suspect was careful not to pull everything out because she wanted the victim to think that the bank bag contained thousands of dollars in bills. As the suspect continued her scam, she reached inside the bank bag and retrieved what appeared to be a bond of some type. The suspect told the victim that this was probably drug money and that she would share the funds with the victim. The suspect told the victim that she knew of an attorney who could assist them in the process. The victim agreed to drive the suspect to meet the attorney.

The victim and the suspect drove to another location and met with a second suspect who was male. The female suspect told the victim that this person was a good friend of hers and that he was an attorney. Playing the part of an attorney, the second suspect listened intently as the first suspect and victim explained what they had found. The second suspect then unzipped the bank bag and told the victim that the bag contained approximately 3 million dollars in currency and bonds. The second suspect told the victim that for them to claim the contents of the bank bag, a lot of money would be needed for taxes and legal fees. The elderly lady began to make extremely large withdrawals from her accounts. After making the withdrawals, the elderly lady would meet with the suspects and give them the money. When just about all of the money had been withdrawn from her accounts and given to the suspects, the suspects disappeared. The victim lost an extremely large amount of money to these two fraud perpetrators. The victim's family discovered the incident a few weeks later and filed a police report. The case had very few leads which were dead ends. A composite drawing of the female suspect was compiled which reflected a possible likeness. The story was shown on the local news channels and passed along the law enforcement network. Neither of the two suspects was ever identified and both are still at large. The fraud perpetrators were able to defraud the victim of this case out of several hundred thousands of dollars.

One tip that anyone can use to prevent being victimized by a pigeon drop scam is to report all found property to their local police department. The con man or woman, for obvious reasons, will not want to involve the police. This will be an automatic indicator that the scam is illegal. In fact, many states have enacted laws regarding the theft of lost or mislaid property and people have been arrested and charged with a criminal offense because they were in possession of the article or articles. People have often heard phrases such as "finders, keepers" and "possession is nine tenths of the law" but the truth is that found property belongs to the original owner. Whenever anyone finds something of value, it is important that every attempt be made to locate the original owner. The first step, in this process, is to contact the local police department, file a police report, and then have the police department take custody of the found article(s). After this initial first step, the person or persons who found the lost property can take additional steps to claim the lost property if the original owner is not located.

If by chance, you are ever approached by someone with a deal that is too good to believe, keep your guard up. It is quite possibly one of these scams commonly referred to as a pigeon drop. Keep your hard earned money. Remember just about all good things take time. An old song from the seventies had a verse that comes to mind, "A fool and his money soon go their separate way." Think twice and three times, if necessary, before ever letting go of your hard earned cash. Pigeon drop fraud perpetrators rely on the victim's greed and the opportunity to make a lot of money fast. Growing up, I would often hear the phrase, "There's a sucker born everyday". Do not let yourself become victimized by such scams.

Chapter Nineteen

The Office Manager: Employer's Beware

In my career, I have investigated many cases and several have involved dishonest employees working for individuals and businesses. I will describe two such cases that I was able to obtain enough information to exact arrests for the perpetrators. There are numerous other cases regarding dishonest employees and I will refer to those in other chapters.

The first case involved an office manager for a doctor's office who had obtained the position through a temp agency. The doctor's thriving practice relied upon referrals and she received payments directly from the insurance companies in the form of checks made payable to her practice.

The suspect, who was employed as the office manager, impressed the doctor so much during her temporary period; the doctor hired her permanently for that position. The office manager's position required the suspect to do a lot of tasks such as answering the telephone, making appointments, and assisting in keeping the books. It was the latter that proved too much of a temptation for the suspect. As the insurance checks came in to the doctor's office, the suspect was to log each check, stamp each check for deposit only with the doctor's corporate checking account number, take the checks to the doctor's local bank branch, and then deposit each check into the doctor's account.

The doctor had her taxes completed by her tax attorney and accountant. An internal audit of the doctor's business revealed a deficit exceeding $100,000. As the doctor and her tax attorney began to investigate the loss of revenue, they discovered that numerous checks had not been deposited into her corporate account. The doctor, her tax attorney, and her accountant began to investigate the missing funds and checks. After obtaining several copies of checks from various insurance companies, they discovered that some of the insurance checks had not been logged into the business ledger and discovered that these checks had been cashed instead of being deposited into her corporate account. They also discovered that these particular checks contained the stamped signature of the doctor. The doctor, tax attorney, and accountant suspected that the office manager had intentionally neglected to log the checks and then proceeded to cash these checks using the doctor's stamped signature pad.

The doctor's tax attorney and accountant came to the Major Fraud office to file a police report and speak with a detective concerning the case. After taking the report, I began the investigation. I began by interviewing the doctor and advising her that copies of all of the compromised checks needed to be obtained as I was conducting the investigation. The doctor was afraid that the suspect would flee if she terminated her employment so the doctor decided to keep her employed but the doctor and her attorney took over the responsibility of all financial transactions. After obtaining all of the necessary evidence which provided me with sufficient Probable Cause, I obtained arrest warrants for the suspect.

After gaining sufficient Probable Cause and the arrest warrants, I arrested the suspect at the physician's office. The suspect was advised of her Constitutional Rights at the time of the arrest but she waived those Rights and agreed to speak with me without an attorney present.

During the interrogation, I questioned the suspect about the incidents. When I asked the question, "Did you cash checks written to the doctor's business for cash?" she responded "Yes, but at the doctor's orders." After the interview had concluded, the suspect was transported to the detention center and processed. I then contacted the physician concerning the suspect's allegations. The doctor was furious when she discovered what the suspect had told me.

After transporting the suspect to the detention center, I placed subpoenas for the production of evidence to the suspect's banking institution for her bank records. The suspect was making approximately $805.00 net every two weeks as an office manager for the physician's office. Her bank records indicated that she had made cash deposits into the account at the tune of approximately $5000.00 to $6000.00 per month.

The second case also involved an office manager, who had obtained the position through the "gift of gab". The suspect was able to befriend the owner and gain his confidence. As usual, the suspect began by impressing the business owner with his work ethic and attitude. The suspect was in charge of all of the office workings which included a lot of the financial doings. The owner of the business was so impressed and befriended that he gave the suspect a charge card in the suspect's name on the corporate account. This is often done by a business so that the employee can make purchases necessary for the operation of the business without constantly bothering those who own and/or operate the business.

The suspect began to use his corporate charge for his own personal use. He ran up a pretty good tab on the account while at the same time destroying the bills which were coming in to the business. The suspect became very greedy and even used a charge card in the name of the owner of the business. The owner discovered the incidents after he had been contacted by a collection agency attempting to recover the debt. Upon discovering that he was in debt a tremendous amount of money, the owner confronted the suspect about the incident. The suspect immediately quit and moved out of his apartment. The owner then contacted the Major Fraud office, filed a police report, and I began the investigation.

After obtaining a statement from the victim and acquiring evidence of the charges made upon the two charge cards, I obtained arrest warrants for the suspect. Our Fugitive Unit was able to track the suspect to an extended stay hotel in another jurisdiction and exact the arrest.

The suspect was charged with financial transaction card fraud and theft by taking. Prior to this case, the suspect had spent a great deal of his life behind bars for fraud related crimes. Sadly, the owner of the business had to file bankruptcy and is no longer in business. This is one example of how someone's deceit and greed can destroy someone's life.

In regards to employers who hire individuals as their office managers or hire someone to manage the finances, I would highly recommend that a background check be completed by a reliable company. The suspects in the previous cases each had something in common with one another. To begin with, both suspects had an extensive criminal history in fraud related criminal activity and both had served time for their previous crimes. These two suspects also gained the victim's trust and friendship prior to committing any crimes.

This type of crime will continue because of the nature of the beast. Employers are constantly looking for someone that is hard working, trustworthy, and reliable. Con men and women thrive on being able to gain the confidence of their victims. Without this confidence, the con man or woman cannot deceive or defraud.

Chapter Twenty

Consumer Fraud

Have you ever wondered how some types of employment carry an association with fraudulent criminal activities or scams? It is mainly because so many citizens have been cheated, shafted, and abused by many of these dishonest business people throughout the years. As I have mentioned several times, a fraud perpetrator can be anyone however some types of employment seem to have more than their fair share.

Although not as common as it used to be, some used car dealers would "roll" back the odometer of a vehicle to give the impression that the vehicle was not driven as much as it was and to increase the price of the vehicle. Used car prices are set using the vehicle's condition, extra features, and mileage. Reducing the vehicle's mileage was a sure fire way of increasing the selling price and the possibility of a quicker sale. Numerous investigations throughout the United States led to the arrest of several of these unethical dealers and states have enacted new laws regarding used vehicle purchases and/or trade-ins. Another method of used car dealers was to sell salvaged vehicles or vehicles that had extensive accident histories as one that had not been in any type of accident. Several states have now enacted laws stating that a salvaged vehicle must state so on its title.

People often get caught up in the new vehicle purchase and do not think with their heads. Before ever talking to a sales person, research different vehicles with different dealers. The dealership wants to make as much money as they possibly can. I also suggest that you research the price of your trade-in before ever going to the lot. I once had a dealership offer me about one half of my vehicle's trade-in worth and even after negotiating, I walked out unable to reason with the sales person. Some people will get so caught up in wanting the new vehicle that they make serious mistakes which the dealership will eventually capitalize upon. Not only are the making a good profit from you purchasing the new vehicle, they will make a tremendous profit from your trade- in if they only give you approximately one half of the vehicle's worth. Ever wonder about the marketing gimmicks used by car dealers? On more than one occasion, I have witnessed advertisements for new vehicles, in the newspaper, for an incredibly low price. However, when I get to the dealership it seems that the vehicle has already been sold. I would have loved to investigate these dealerships; however, mere suspicion is never enough.

Have you ever had an insurance company attempt to make you pay for their services even though your policy has expired or you have changed insurance to another company? This is called forced renewal and many states have enacted laws to protect the consumer from such practices. Policies have a termination date and some even have a grace period if not paid by the termination date. Insurance companies will sometimes attempt to report you as being delinquent to a credit reporting agency or attempt to have a collection agency collect the insurance premium. I changed insurance companies once and went to another insurance agency because of better rates. The former insurance company threatened to report me to a collection agency; however, this abruptly stopped after I informed them that this was forced renewal and I would be seeking legal representation. Insurance companies will sometimes try to convince you that even though your policy had expired, the company had given you credit to extend your policy. I wonder exactly how many of these insurance companies would pay for your damages if you had an accident during this period. The best thing to do to prevent any cases of forced renewal is to notify the insurance company, in writing, when you change insurance companies and keep a copy for your records. If the insurance company persists in its actions of forced renewal, you have some record to help you in your fight. Forced renewals are quite common place; especially, when a person signs up for a service and the payment is deducted from the credit card or debit card. Some people find it very hard to stop the services and the payments from being deducted from their accounts even after they notify the business that they no longer wish to be a participant. Is it a case of an honest mistake or is it deceptive business practices? It seems to me that if these are cases of honest mistakes, the business would refund the person's funds back into their accounts.

One form of inappropriate behavior prevalent today is one used by some businesses to generate subscriptions to their magazines or services. This is more of a nuisance for more citizens than the amount of money spent. However, the rewards to businesses doing this type of inappropriate behavior are great. Often, a person will answer an advertisement for a free copy of a magazine, receive the magazine, and then begin to receive subsequent publications. Shortly after, they will receive a bill for an entire year's subscription.

Another form consists of a person purchasing services for a trial period. This type usually requires that the individual purchase the trial services with a credit card. After the trial period has expired, the individual will continue to receive the services and his or her credit card will be billed for the services. Some individuals will contact the business and request that the account be cancelled. Some businesses will immediately comply while others make the cancellation a difficult and tedious process. Some individuals have even had their credit cards billed for services months after the service was cancelled. I would suggest that anyone interested in participating in trial offers such as these complete some research into the business first. This can be accomplished by using an internet search engine and type in something to the effect "cancel subscription to such and such company". If the company is the type as I have described in this paragraph, you will probably discover several people who have had problems and posted their comments. Anyone victimized by a business using inappropriate sales methods should file a complaint with the Federal Trade Commission.

Let the buyer beware. That particular phrase has been in existence a long, long time for a very good reason. Whenever you make a purchase for anything, new or used, use common sense, and completely research what you are buying and where you are purchasing the item or article. There are a lot of fakes and counterfeit stuff out there. Many people have purchased items at flea markets, online auctions, and even in some retail stores, believing that the item was genuine. Counterfeiters have made an art of duplicating the original item and often it is unable to tell the counterfeit from the original, only trained personnel using trade secrets can make that determination in a lot of cases. Ever see that expensive watch or purse being sold for hundreds and sometimes thousands of dollars less than normal? Chances are it could be counterfeit. Be very cautious when purchasing products and use extreme caution when purchasing items unseen as through an internet auction house. Counterfeit items such as bootleg CDs, DVDs, clothing, and jewelry are not of the same quality as the original and are usually smuggled into the United States from another country. This not only presents a problem for our economy but also jeopardizes the original companies. If allowed to continue, counterfeit articles can bankrupt the original company and have a lot of employees left without employment.

Even though consumer protection agencies exist and do their part to protect the rights of consumers, it is everyone's responsibility to do their part to protect themselves. Use caution and diligence whenever making a purchase and try to avoid becoming a victim of consumer fraud.

Chapter Twenty-One

Corporate Fraud

Do you trust your lawyer, banker, or broker? How about the Chief Executive Officer or Chief Financial Officer of your corporation? Just like the rest of the population, fraud perpetrators can be anyone and some of the largest fraudulent crimes have been perpetrated by some employed as such. Large corporate fraud can be devastating to the economy costing millions, even billions, of dollars, lost jobs, and lost savings for many honest and hardworking employees. Fraudulent crimes, for the most part, involve deceit and the theft of currency or some other valuable. Some types of corporate fraud can involve cover ups of criminal incidents and environmental issues. Corporate fraud can and does cause serious problems both economically and environmentally. Corporate fraud has injured, maimed, and even killed.

A look back in history and one can see that some of the largest losses can be attributed to corporate fraud. The Savings and Loan scandal of the eighties cost taxpayers millions if not billions of dollars. Recent corporate fraud like Enron, WorldCom, Adelphia, Tyco, Arthur Anderson, and HealthSouth, for example, has cost everyday Americans billions of dollars. In addition, the honest hardworking employees who had nothing to do with the fraudulent criminal activities of the corporate officers saw their life savings and future go down the drain. Enron executives used deceit and manipulative practices to fraudulently obtain higher stock prices. To accomplish corporate fraud, more than one individual is usually involved making it a conspiracy. One thing about corporate fraudulent criminal acts is that a lot of people, bankers and attorneys, know about the fraudulent crimes but because the business was making enormous profits, at the time, do not blow the whistle. It is often easy for someone to look the other way especially when they stand to gain millions from the fraudulent incident.

Corporate fraud can take on different levels from manipulating or cooking the books to that of cover-ups. Cover-ups often involve a dangerous substance or chemicals which the business uses or produces to manufacture its product. The Environmental Protection Agency or E.P.A. monitors businesses and corporations and laws have been enacted to protect the public and the environment. Problems arise when a corporation which uses a chemical or chemicals with potential health hazards or even the possibility of death and these chemicals are released into the environment. Several large cases in the past years have revealed that a few unscrupulous corporations will attempt to hide any evidence of toxic waste dumping into the environment. These companies have been fined an enormous amount of money for the infractions and families of the victims have won enormous civil judgments against the liable corporations.

Every state has specialized departments or agencies with investigators to oversee each and every attorney. The state's Bar Association oversees any acts of wrong doing and if an attorney is found to be in violation of the state's code and ethics can see his or her license revoked. Attorneys who have been disbarred or placed on probation are listed within each court system. One look at this listing reveals that numerous attorneys, for one reason or another, can no longer practice law legally within the state.

Banking and financial institutions are regulated by both state and federal regulatory agencies. Banks are businesses. If banks do not make money they fail. Most of the time when a person applies for a loan through a financial institution, that person must provide collateral or use enough of their own money to insure that the financial institution will recoup their losses if the loan is defaulted. There have been a lot of cases of high ranking banking officials stealing money from their clients and even stealing a person's residence, land, or other valuable asset. One recent banking institution fraud actually saw the collapse of the institution itself. Speaking with one of the former managers of the business, who had been convicted and spent time in prison with several other managers, I was amazed to hear some of the things that had occurred. The financial institution would often lend money to area farmers in need of new machinery knowing damn well that the farmer would not be able to repay the loan. Since the financial institution would have the farmer place his farm up as collateral, the financial institution was able to obtain valuable land for only pennies on the dollar. I suppose if the farmer had taken a loan in the amount of 80% or 90% of his farm's value and the loan defaulted, it would have been an entirely different story altogether. However, in this case and others, the financial institution would require as collateral the farm and all the equipment for a loan which was only a small percentage of the farm's actual value. It took several years of diligent investigation, but the financial institution was brought down and those responsible for the fraudulent thefts fined and received prison terms.

Most attorneys, financial institutions, and corporations do play by the rules and make a living legally. As with any other profession, there are always exceptions to the rule. If you have been wronged by an attorney, you should contact your state's Bar Association and file a complaint. For banks and other financial institution complaints, contact your state's regulatory agency or even the federal regulatory agency. In cases involving theft or fraud, file a police report with your local, state, or federal agency in addition to filing complaints with your state's regulatory agency or federal regulatory agency.

Almost everyone dreams of finding a new stock which will increase exponentially, over time, turning a modest investment into millions. Some individuals through skillful investment practices, knowledge, or plain luck have made millions in the stock market. For a few though, they attempt to break the rules of investment trading and gain profits through dishonest inside information. Imagine if you have a close personal friend who owns a pharmaceutical company and the friend tells you that next week it will be announced publicly that the company is working toward a cure for major disease. You run right out and purchase as much as the company's stock as you can afford. The following weeks after the company makes its announcement public, their stock soars. After the stock reaches an all time high, the close friend notifies you that the test results for the new experimental drug are negative and the news will be released to the public within a few days. After receiving this news, you contact your broker and sell off all of your holdings in your friends' corporation making you a lot of money. After the business goes public with the negative results, the corporation's stock then drops to what it was previously. You made a lot of money while others lost. The money made was not the result of skillful and honest investment practices but rather through slick and underhanded practices. A profit was made through an unfair and illegal advantage.

The white collar criminal associated with corporate fraud usually does not receive their just punishment for the tremendous crimes and pain that they cause others. Some receive a little jail time and most will keep their homes and a lot of their assets. I, for one, believe that criminals such as these should receive the maximum sentence and lose everything just like the honest and hard working victims had their savings stolen or reduced to a small fraction of what they once had. The punishment should fit the crime.

Chapter Twenty-Two

Employee Thefts and Fraudulent Acts

Thefts committed by employees can cost a business dearly and sometimes, as in the case of the office manager, can be catastrophic to the business and cause its collapse into bankruptcy. Many large chains have loss prevention or asset protection managers and employees that keep a watchful eye out for their employees and their customers. Still, employees can and will commit crimes which encompass everything from simple shoplifting to embezzlement.

A few years ago, I worked a case involving a sales person for a major hotel in Atlanta. The person was responsible for obtaining contracts from large businesses and corporations coming in to Atlanta for conventions. Usually, the contracts were drawn for a specific booking of between 100 to 300 rooms and between 3 to 7 days at a time. In a matter of speaking, that meant that the bookings involved between 300 room rentals up to 2100 room rentals each and every time. The sales person would receive a bonus check every time she booked a group or business. The bonus was paid to the salesperson at the time of the booking not at the actual date of the booking.

The suspect began to book future events by fabricating paperwork with forged signatures to make the paperwork appear legitimate. The suspect did several of these over a period of a few years. During that time, she received about $111,000 in bonuses. Prior to the date of the first fraudulent booking event, the suspect resigned her position with the hotel and left. The hotel began to realize that something was terribly wrong when the first booking date arrived and no one from the business arrived. The hotel began to look into this booking and discovered that the business had arranged to have their convention in another city and state. With this discovery, the hotel's sales staff began to contact other businesses that the ex-sales person had booked. That is how everything came to light.

To build the case, I had to retrieve records from the hotel's legal staff and obtain copies of the documents which had been submitted fraudulently on each and every bogus contract. All of these businesses were located throughout the United States and making contact with the appropriate personnel for each business took some time. After contacting each and every business, I had to obtain written statements from those people whose signatures had been forged and from the people who actually had the final say on the contracts. After obtaining all of these documents and statements, I obtained felony arrest warrants for the suspect's arrest. She was arrested shortly thereafter.

The suspect was able to steal over $111,000.00 in bonus checks by fraudulently submitting bogus contracts. The hotel's loss of revenue, however, from these fraudulent contracts was staggering. I was given an estimate at well over 1 million dollars for that figure. I am sure that they were able to recover some of that estimated loss though, since the dates of some of those fraudulent contracts had not yet transpired. I don't know if the hotel placed new operating procedures regarding bonus pay or if they just decided to keep a more watchful eye on their employees by verifying such contracts.

Just about all fraud detectives have, at one time or another, worked different variations of employee thefts. In Georgia, these thefts are commonly known as theft-by-conversion cases because the suspect is simply converting cash or merchandise that rightfully belongs to the business to their own personal use.

As an officer and then as a detective, I worked numerous such theft-by-conversion cases. Sometimes, the suspect would remove currency from the cash register and place the currency inside of their pants pocket or purse. At other times, the suspect would be working the register when a friend or family member approached with a buggy full of merchandise or groceries. The suspect would deliberately bag some items without scanning the items and the family member or friend would often leave the store with a large amount of merchandise without paying for most of it. Individual incidents of this nature may not appear to be much of a loss at the time, but continued incidents throughout the dishonest employee's length of service can be quite costly to the employer.

Sometimes, criminal acts such as theft by shoplifting can take on a fraudulent atmosphere. One such case involved a suspect who had made numerous purchases of vacuum cleaners valued at about $500 or more each. This individual would purchase these expensive vacuum cleaners for the price of a vacuum cleaner of lesser quality. The suspect would travel around the Atlanta area and purchase three or four of these vacuum cleaners at each location. He would usually make 8 to 12 purchases every few days. The Asset

Protection Manager became aware of the theft and began to investigate the suspect.

The suspect would place counterfeit UPC labels on the more expensive vacuum cleaners which would reflect a lower price. He or an accomplice would enter stores, a day, or two in advance, and place these counterfeit UPC labels on the more expensive cleaners. He would then exit the store and return on another date to purchase every cleaner in the store. If stopped at the register, he would play dumb. Asset Protection was never really able to obtain video surveillance of the suspect placing the UPC labels on the cleaners because he did it so far in advance or either had an accomplice do it for him. Most large department stores will not chance a law suit on making an arrest on a suspect if investigative methods are not met such as witnessed incidents or video surveillance.

The Asset Protection Manager built an extremely good case against the suspect. She was able to show that the suspect had visited several stores, throughout Georgia, in a short period of time, and had made purchases of several expensive cleaners at each store. The suspect made his home north of Atlanta and through the diligent work of the Asset Protection Manager, a search warrant for the suspect's residence was obtained by the police agency where the suspect resided. The search warrant proved to be invaluable in the recovery of numerous stolen vacuum cleaners and other merchandise. Also recovered were the counterfeit UPC labels which the suspect was placing on the more expensive cleaners.

The suspect would purchase these expensive cleaners at about a tenth of their cost using this method. He would then resell the cleaners at an online auction, making a tremendous profit on each one. The Asset Protection Manager did an excellent job on this one and saved the business thousands of dollars.

Another interesting case did not actually involve the employee of that particular business but the employee of another business. Stores will provide certain services to individuals who, for one reason or another, can not make it in to the store to shop. In this particular incident, an elderly lady contacted the Asset Protection Manager of the store wishing to make several purchases for her children and grand children for Christmas. The lady purchased several gift cards from the business and paid for the cards using her credit card. The Asset Protection Manager activated the gift cards, addressed each one per the lady's request, and then mailed the cards.

A few days prior to Christmas, the lady contacted the store and spoke with the Asset Protection Manager. The lady explained that she had telephoned her children and grand children to see if they had received the gift cards and they had told her that they had not. The Asset Protection Manager reviewed the store's program and located each number for each gift card. When he ran the gift card numbers through his system, he discovered that each of the gift cards had been redeemed at his store. The Asset Protection Manager began reviewing the video surveillance tapes and he was astonished at his discovery. He immediately notified me and I responded to the store to view the video surveillance.

The video surveillance revealed that the cards had been redeemed for merchandise. The astonishing fact was that this suspect was wearing an United States Postal uniform. An Inspector from the United States Postal Inspections Services was notified and began the investigation. The Postal Inspector obtained the video surveillance tapes of this incident and also purchased two additional gift cards which were recorded and then mailed from the business location to a person in his office. The Inspector captured, on video surveillance, the suspect picking up the postal mailings and then later on that day, redeeming the gift cards at the business. The suspect was arrested for the theft and also lost her job. It has never ceased to amaze me how some people will risk a very good job to commit crimes, especially crimes such as this.

The last employee involved a person that I had known and made cases with over the years. This case really bothered me a lot but needed to be investigated. The employee in question was the loss prevention manager for a large department store in Atlanta. He had noticed a female enter the store and make a purchase for a $500 gift card. He knew that the female had been in the store before and suspected that she had purchased gift cards using stolen and altered checks. As he delayed the transaction to investigate this incident, he contacted the owner of the check who confirmed the check as stolen. The loss prevention manager then detained the female suspect and notified the Atlanta Police of the incident. The suspect was arrested and transported to jail. The check was seized as evidence and the $500 gift card was returned to the loss prevention manager to be deactivated.

The problem arose when the loss prevention manager did not deactivate the $500 gift card. Instead, he took the card and paid on his business credit card debt and made a few purchases for some clothing. The district office discovered the incident and attempted to question him regarding the theft. He refused to answer any questions and left the business. The district manager then came to my office to file a police report and to begin the investigation. After obtaining statements and other items of evidence, I obtained an arrest warrant for someone that I had known and trusted for several years. I attempted to have him turn himself in to me at my office but he would not cooperate. He was eventually arrested by another jurisdiction completing a traffic stop. I never really got a chance to ask him why he did this and I can only speculate.

Chapter Twenty-Three

The Fake Employment Scam

If confidence men or con men are anything, they are very ingenious and imaginative. One such con artist created a scam which he deceived about a dozen people and took them for about $30,000. In this devious scam, the con artist did a little research of a particular internet business that dealt with the automotive industry and obtained the checking account information of several car dealers in the area. The con artist then ran an advertisement in the local paper which read something like this: Large internet based business seeking highly motivated people for sales representative positions. Salary of $35k with bonuses to $70k, health, dental, and life. 401k. etc. Please call XXX-XXX-XXXX.

I don't know how many people actually responded to the advertisement; however, the con artist picked about a dozen people to interview and scam. All of the people were told to meet him in a hotel conference room. He had obtained a golf shirt with the name of the business imprinted on it and had the business name imprinted on all of the paperwork. Each of the victims were given an application which they completed, given paperwork describing the company's standard operating procedures and benefits, and then subjected to an interview conducted by the con artist.

The suspect interviewed the victims on several occasions at three different hotels. During the last interview, the suspect told each of the victims that they had been offered employment and that they needed to submit to him a deposit slip for their checking account because the company did not issue payroll checks but only paid via direct deposit.

After that meeting with the victims, the suspect then deposited counterfeit checks made on the accounts of area automotive dealers into each of the victim's checking accounts using the deposit slips that each victim had provided. He had copied the appearance of each of the dealer's checks complete with the name, address, and account numbers. The checks had all been made payable to the victims and had been written for either $2,500 or $4,000. I never have figured out why he chose these amounts and why he didn't do all of the checks in the same amount. I guess the suspect had his reasons.

After depositing the counterfeit checks into each victim's checking account, the suspect telephoned each victim and told them that he had just been informed that the large internet based business had just enacted a new advertising procedure and that the business had just made a deposit of $2,500 or $4,000 into each of their checking accounts. He then advised each victim that they needed to withdraw the funds from their banking institution in increments of $100 bills. The suspect told each victim that these one hundred dollar bills were to be used by the victim as part of an advertisement plan and that the funds were to be given to each potential customer just for their time. The suspect had each victim meet him at an area hotel and give him the currency. After receiving the funds, the suspect told each victim that he had compiled a list of perspective customers and that the following day would be their "training day". The suspect advised each victim to dress appropriately, women would wear nice dresses and men should wear a suit. The victims were all advised to meet back at the hotel the following morning at 9:00 A.M.

The following morning, all of the victims met in the hotel's conference room waiting on the suspect to arrive. The suspect never appeared and during the wait, one victim received a telephone call from his banking institution advising him that the check which had been deposited into his account was counterfeit and that he needed to come into the bank immediately. The remaining victims then began to contact their banking institutions and, one by one, discovered that the checks which the suspect had deposited into their checking accounts were counterfeit.

I contacted the large internet business and spoke with their vice president concerning the suspect. The business advised that they did not have any person by the suspect's name in their employment nor did they ever have anyone employed by that name. The business was not currently seeking sales representatives and did not have any active recruiters in the Atlanta area.

All of the victims had been faced with an emotional roller coaster. First, they thought that they had landed a tremendous employment opportunity which paid well and had great benefits. Most, if not all, of the victims were currently unemployed and most had families to support. Then, they discover that the job that they thought they had obtained did not exist. The final devastating blow to the victims came when they discovered that they had to repay the funds which the suspect had instructed them to withdraw from their bank accounts in increments of $100 bills.

Banking institutions will often take the loss on counterfeit checks passed through a person's account; however, in this case, because the victim actually withdrew the funds in person, they held the account holder responsible for repaying the funds.

I exhausted every method of investigation on this case trying to identify and arrest the suspect responsible. To me, this was one of the most horrendous cases of fraud that I have ever experienced. It is always terrible when people are defrauded and have something stolen from them but it is horrible when people have their emotions played with and their hopes lifted and then destroyed. Then to top it all off to find out that they are now responsible for repaying something that they really couldn't afford to be repaying.

As I mentioned, I exhausted every investigative technique attempting to solve this crime. The only thing that I did not do was to air the case on the local television news programs. I had video surveillance footage from the hotels and banking institutions but had no clue as to who the perpetrator was.

The suspect resurfaced in a jurisdiction just north of Atlanta about nine months later running a similar scam which involved giving the victim counterfeit checks. The detective, in that case, immediately obtained video surveillance photographs and aired the video surveillance photographs on a local news program. A citizen watching the news program recognized the suspect's picture and knew that he was staying at an extended stay hotel in another part of metro Atlanta. This citizen called the police and the detectives and officers from the two jurisdictions responded to the location of the extended stay hotel. The suspect was apprehended and his true identity was discovered. The suspect had an U.S. Marshall's warrant for his arrest, a felony arrest warrant out of Texas, and I was now able to obtain felony warrants for his arrest on 30 plus counts of forgery and theft by deception.

Most fraud perpetrators do not receive a lot of jail time but this guy will be the exception. This suspect had prior felony convictions, committed several felonies in different jurisdictions, and played upon the emotions and feelings of his victims. This suspect could very well spend the rest of his life in prison.

People can avoid becoming victims of such a scam by doing a little investigative work of their own prior to and during such a scam. The business should have a contact number and a home office somewhere. Locate this telephone number through your own investigation, never use the telephone number that the suspect gives you. Contact the business and inquire about the person claiming to be from their Human Resources Department. In this case, the business would have told each victim that no one by that name was employed by the company and a red flag would have appeared. Second, if a business is seeking employees in the area they will obtain an office locally or they will use the same hotel. If locations keep changing, a red flag should go up. Finally, use common sense and don't let the suspect's gift of gab convince you of something your gut instinct is telling you not to do. Think first, and then act. Companies are in the business of making money, if they don't they will not be in business for long. I don't know of any successful business which gives money to a perfect stranger without first getting something from that person. Promotional advertisements are always in the form of checks or some other type of document which can be redeemed at a later date by the receiver. If someone tells you that funds have just been deposited into your account, for whatever reason, and then tells you that you need to withdraw those funds and then give them to him or her, a red flag should immediately appear in your head.

Chapter Twenty-Four

Government Fraud

One case that I investigated involved some deceptive and fraudulent transactions involving two employees of the city of Atlanta who had victimized a bunch of citizens. The case took a long time to investigate before the two employees were arrested for their crimes.

The two employees came up with a scheme to defraud numerous victims who had fallen behind on their water bill. The two suspects were placed in the collections department and would contact those citizens and complexes when their water bills became past due. The individuals began to call these citizens telling them that their water bill was about to be disconnected unless an immediate payment was brought to the water department. The suspects told numerous victims that the city would accept a settlement offer which was usually one quarter to one third of the outstanding bill. Whenever anyone would attempt to pay by a credit card, personal check, or money order, the employees would tell them that the settlement offer was valid only if paid in cash.

Each of the victims was advised to bring the currency down to city hall and give the currency directly to one of the suspects. Several victims requested a receipt for their payment and the suspects obliged.

After each victim had paid cash money to the suspects for the settlement of the outstanding water bill, the two employees would construct a new account for the victim's address. The suspects did not have the capability to remove the previous outstanding debt but did have the ability to generate new accounts in the system. The previous accounts, however, were still in the system and were found during an audit.

The case began when a victim who had been approached by the two suspects paid the so-called settlement. The individuals had failed to enter a new account in the system and the victim's services were disconnected. The victim complained to the mayor's office who, in turn, contacted the city's legal department and water department. This initial complaint opened up a much larger fraud investigation and that is when the case was turned over to the Major Fraud office for investigation. Before our investigation commenced, the two employees had been terminated for other reasons. After months of investigation into the incidents, arrest warrants were obtained for the two former employees and they were arrested shortly thereafter.

Speaking of deceit and fraud in government, numerous cases have come to light throughout the years as politicians and government employees have been indicted and arrested on fraud related criminal charges and betraying the public's trust. Atlanta is no different from several other large cities in the United States. Not long ago, a former mayor of Atlanta was indicted by a Federal Grand Jury on racketeering and tax evasion charges. The jury did convict him of tax evasion but did not convict him of the other charges. Numerous others in his administration had already pleaded guilty to corruption.

For those of you who may not know this, when the AUSA or Attorney for the United States of America takes on a case, it is done completely and correctly. No stone will be left unturned and every piece of evidence will be obtained. Only after all the evidence is obtained and all of the witnesses and suspects are interviewed will the case proceed to a Federal Grand Jury. If there is the slightest doubt in the case, the AUSA will not proceed. In other words, they complete an air tight case based on evidence. The only way a defense attorney or a team of defense attorneys can defeat a case such as this is to argue points of the case with the deliberate attempt to place doubt in the mind of at least one juror. I love the law and believe in due process. But it seems to me that a lot of trials, especially those involving celebrities and political figures, have become a stage. The attorneys have become actors and cases are often decided upon their acting ability rather than the evidence at hand.

I was a patrol officer during the former mayor's terms. My job and that of other officers was to serve and to protect. A patrol officer is pretty much a person who is the jack of all trades, so to speak. An officer will patrol a particular section or beat of town looking for any criminal activity while at the same time deterring the activity. He or she will respond to 911 emergency calls, provide life saving techniques, handle accident situations, disturbances of the peace, handle domestic violence situations, take reports on criminal activity, and work traffic. An officer working traffic looks for individuals who are speeding, driving recklessly, or in some other ways breaking traffic laws.

Before an officer can attempt a traffic stop, they must have sufficient Probable Cause, Reasonable Articulable Suspicion, or witness the person driving the vehicle commit some type of traffic offense. An officer working traffic can prevent a lot of accidents from occurring but it can also be a great investigative tool. Officers have captured every type of criminal through traffic stops. Sometimes, a suspect will drive erratically after leaving the scene of a crime and be stopped by an officer and arrested. Other incidents have seen the officer complete a traffic stop and after running a wants/warrants check on the occupant discover that the person has felony warrants for a particular criminal act. Traffic is necessary and is definitely a part of each patrol officer's daily routine. Many larger jurisdictions, such as Atlanta, have specialized motor units to work traffic because of the mass volume of motorists.

As most people are aware, a traffic violation can be costly. Depending on the offense, traffic fines can be between $20 and over $1,000 or more. The theory behind the fines is that people will learn from their mistakes if made to pay for them. This is a basic concept that we all learn as children. A child might touch a hot stove once but the pain will serve as a reminder to the child the rest of his or her life.

Problems arise, however, since many jurisdictions have discovered that they benefit from traffic cases. The city or jurisdiction will receive the fines which can be used at their discretion. People have heard of some jurisdictions being nicknamed speed traps. Officers of these jurisdictions are ordered to run radar or laser in high traffic areas and their sole job is to write tickets which generate the city money. In Atlanta, officers were told that they needed to write at least two tickets per day and sometimes, depending on which zone or area an officer patrolled, it increased to five per day. Officers were threatened with having their regular off days taken away or being removed from their beat cars if they didn't comply. Several attempts were made to base an officer's step or annual increase in pay on factors which primarily included traffic enforcement.

No jurisdiction will openly admit to any type of quota system but just about all have an unwritten policy to the effect. Do not get me wrong, there are drivers that need to be cited because of their dangerous driving habits. People often drive too fast, follow too closely, and present a danger to everyone else on the roadway. I do have a problem when jurisdictions place more emphasis on traffic and very little emphasis of fighting and detouring criminal activity. During this particular time, the city of Atlanta was overwhelmed with criminal incidents. During this period, the city of Atlanta always ranked in the top 5 meanest cities in America. Patrol officers were given orders to bring in traffic tickets which made the city money. An officer who wrote a lot of traffic citations had things a little bit easier than the officer who concentrated on his or her particular beat. At that time, it seemed as though the majority of officers were ordered to bring in more and more traffic citations to appease those downtown. During this former mayor's administration, officers were attempting to bargain for better pay. Many officers were just getting by and just about every officer had to moonlight to survive. Union discussions with the former mayor and his administration ended abruptly. Since police officers cannot strike, the union called for a slow down. This slow down was not intended to affect officers responding to emergency calls or from doing their job. This slow down had one thing in mind, which was to curtail the number of traffic tickets generated by officers for the city. Officers would still write traffic tickets but only to those that were committing the most serious of traffic violations. The slow down was scheduled for a Friday.

That day, the former mayor vowed to break the "Blue Flu" and had every supervisor conduct road blocks with their personnel. For those of you that do not know what a road block is, it is a method of traffic enforcement that jurisdictions will use to check drivers for their license, insurance, and registration. Road blocks are a great tool for any agency and community. Road blocks conducted in an area subjected to numerous burglaries and robberies have captured perpetrators attempting to enter the area to commit a crime or leave the area after the crime. Road blocks conducted by jurisdictions have also discovered and arrested many individuals who were driving under the influence of alcohol or drugs presenting a danger to everyone on the roadway. As I have mentioned, road blocks are a tremendous tool for law enforcement agencies but all road blocks must be conducted in accordance with the Fourth Amendment and state laws. Road blocks should never be used to obtain tickets which generate funds for the city, county, or state.

The supervisors had the majority of his or her watch on these road blocks for most of their shifts, leaving only a few officers to patrol the area and answer 911 emergency calls. The officers on the road blocks did not write many traffic tickets; however, the supervisors were the ones who wrote the majority of the tickets produced that day. On the evening news that night, the former mayor gave a news conference claiming that he had broken the 'Blue Flu". He claimed that because of his orders, the police department had written over 100 more tickets than they usually did on a normal Friday. This produced the city money and citizens, because of his actions that day, were left less protected. The bottom line is that it is every officer's duty to serve and protect the public, not generate funds for the city, county, and/or state.

Police officials are always under the gun, so to speak. They are constantly under pressure from political officials to either reduce the crime rate or generate funds for the city or county general fund. Whenever this occurs, officers are forced to work harder in an attempt to please their superiors. Often this will lead an officer to do things that he or she may not have done previously. It could mean the officer making a criminal case even though Probable Cause does not exist, taking shortcuts to police procedures such as thorough investigation, or perhaps issuing a traffic citation that might otherwise not have been written. Officers that fail to comply with these orders and produce are often faced with internal disciplinary actions. Police departments always retain the right to place an employee wherever they want, dictate watches or shifts, and dictate the employee's scheduled off days.

It is imperative that an officer follow orders but it is more important that an officer abide by the laws of their state and the Constitution of the United States of America. Many public officials and a lot of appointed officials like to believe that they are the "boss" of police officers but a police officer has only one true "boss" which is the Constitution of the United States especially the first ten amendments which are known as the Bill of Rights.

Some people enter public office for the right reasons. They believe that they can help others and their community. To right the wrongs and make living better, safer, and easier. Too often, many people enter public office for the wrong reasons, power, and money. Officials will often obtain an office but secretly have a "what's in it for me" attitude. This nation needs and deserves good, honest, and qualified people who are doing things for the right reasons not the wrong ones.

Chapter Twenty-Five

Contractor Fraud and Home Improvement Fraud

At one time or another, just about every home owner needs to make repairs or upgrades to their home. Some people take on the task themselves unless the task is too large, time consuming, or beyond their expertise. When this occurs, many people seek trained personnel such as contractors, carpenters, plumbers, electricians, and painters to complete the job for them. All legitimate contractors, sub contractors, carpenters, plumbers, roofers, electricians, and painters take pride in their work and will usually do the best job that they are capable of. There are those, however, that may not know what they are doing and attempt to convince the home owner that for a certain price they can complete the job within the specified amount of time. I have seen work performed by those qualified and work performed by those not so qualified. There is no comparison between the two. For the most part, the qualified person will build or repair the work correctly and to city, county, or state code. The unqualified person often does not know what code means.

I worked a couple of cases involving contractor fraud as a detective. One particular case involved an individual who wanted to remodel his home by having some siding replaced and a front porch installed. The gentleman located a contractor and the contractor gave him an estimate for the work including labor and materials. The amount was close to $25,000 and the home owner gave the contractor an advanced payment of $5,000 to begin the work. After receiving the $5,000, the contractor began the job and immediately tore the existing siding off of the house. The contractor then told the home owner that he needed the additional money to complete the job and pay for the materials. The home owner immediately issued a check for the remaining amount to the contractor to complete the job.

The home owner became frustrated after several weeks had passed and the contractor had not returned to his home to complete the job. The home owner had attempted to contact the contractor by telephone several times without success and even drove to the contractor's place of residence only to discover that the contractor did not reside at the location. The home owner came into the fraud office to file a police report for the fraud.

After making the police report, the home owner proceeded to write a demand letter stating that the contractor should return to finish the job for the agreed price or return the home owner's funds. The demand letter gave the contractor a generous amount of time to answer the home owner's demands. The home owner made copies of the demand letter for his own records and for further use in a criminal hearing. The demand letter was sent via certified mail addressed to the contractor at his last known place of residence. The home owner, in the mean time, began to make several calls to the telephone numbers provided to him by the contractor. The home owner documented each telephone call, kept a log of all activities, and after he received notification that the letter had been delivered to the suspect's last known residence and giving the suspect ample time to respond, the home owner gathered all of his evidence and proceeded with criminal charges against the contractor. Although not all states may have a specific criminal offense for contractor fraud, there is usually some criminal charge that may apply.

Warrants were obtained for the suspect and I could find no evidence, whatsoever, that the suspect was a legitimate contractor. Only that he had pretended to be a contractor, took the victim's money, and then left the victim with a mess. Our fugitive unit was able to apprehend the suspect in another jurisdiction and he was brought to justice. The so called contractor had defrauded the home owner and it is very doubtful that the home owner was able to recoup any of his losses.

Contracts are generally civil in nature; however, in the state of Georgia for instance, some can turn into a criminal case just like a personal check returned because of insufficient funds can. In this particular case, the so called contractor wasn't a contractor at all and his sole goal was to defraud the home owner of his money. Disagreements often arise between a home owner and the contractor or sub contractor. Disagreements such as these are normally settled between individuals or perhaps settled in a civil court case. If this so called contractor was a legitimate contractor, he would probably have answered the home owner's requests and this case would have been resolved civilly.

The second case involved a home owner who had hired an individual to complete some work to her fire damaged home. The suspect was already under investigation for mortgage fraud when this lady came into the fraud office to file a complaint. The home owner had obtained the services of this so called contractor to repair her damaged home. She had to obtain another residence while the work was being completed and after the work was completed, moved back into her residence. The home owner began to experience several problems within her home after she moved back in. Doors and windows would not shut. The floor began to sag. The home owner took pictures of the repair work and it revealed that the suspect had used 2 x4's for the floor joists and one can only wonder if any headers were re-installed above the windows and doors in the bearing walls.

This so-called contractor did not follow codes which have been established for safety purposes and it was evident that no building permits were ever issued because no building inspector would ever pass the work. One thing to remember when hiring someone to do some work on your home or business is look at their previous jobs and talk with the home owners concerning the contractors work. Reputable contractors will gladly give you several references for their work. Also, make sure that if your city or county requires permits before construction or remodeling that you obtain them before any work is done.

When I was growing up, numerous home owners were defrauded by illegal tactics of sales people. One such fraud was the siding industry. Home owners are always looking for a siding material that requires little or no maintenance and looks good. Unethical siding companies hired sales people to generate business for their companies by offering free siding to home owners. The scam went something like this. A sales person would knock on the door of a home owner and deliver their sales pitch when the home owner answered the door. The sales person would often pick poor and uneducated people. The sales person would explain to this home owner that the siding would be free. The sales person never mentioned that there was a charge to install the siding. After the home owner signed the contract, a siding contractor for the business arrived and installed the siding. After the installation of the siding, the home owner would receive an enormous bill for the labor charges. The scam took a lot of home owners until local, state, and federal agencies stepped in. The old saying if it sounds too good to be true, it probably isn't true would be very appropriate for this type of scam.

Whenever you are considering remodeling your residence or perhaps adding an addition to your residence, research your contractors and sub contractors thoroughly. Don't be afraid to ask questions and talk to other people and home owners about their contractors or sub contractors. A quality contractor or sub contractor will welcome these questions and will gladly give you references for their work.

On the flip side of coin, if you hire someone to complete work for you on your residence or building and the work is completed as agreed and to code be sure to pay the contractor and sub contractors for their work. Too often, people will try to get free labor, services, and materials by attempting to avoid payments for the work. People will sometimes attempt to avoid paying for services or work because they are not satisfied with the work completed. First, there is a fine line here between what is civil and what is criminal. For example, if a person enters a restaurant, orders a meal, and then eats the meal they are responsible for payment even though they might not have liked the meal. If you are dissatisfied with what you have ordered or perhaps the way it was cooked, ask to speak to the manager. Most restaurants will try to please the patron.

If you hire someone to complete work on your home or business, whether it is cleaning or remodeling, and the contractor or sub contractor completes the work, they must be paid for their services although the home owner may not be completely satisfied with the quality of work. Some people expect too much and expect to see things in better than new condition after the service. The home owner has two options. First, they can attempt to settle the disagreement with the owner or manager of the business and if that does not work, they can pursue a civil suit in a court of law seeking reimbursement of their funds. A person refusing payment to any establishment or business that has rendered services may be subjected to an arrest depending on the circumstances. State codes usually have a charge for anyone attempting to avoid such payments. Most reputable and legitimate businesses will make every attempt to please their customers because the survival of their business is based on satisfied customers. Businesses that provide a below average level of customer service usually are not in business long.

Chapter Twenty-Six

Insurance Fraud

Insurance fraud occurs every day and often is not caught by insurance companies or brought to the attention of law enforcement. Several people have discovered that they can receive funds from the insurance agency by making bogus claims on a legitimate insurance claim such as the case regarding a burglary to a residence. The victim may feel the temptation to report something as stolen that, in fact, had not been stolen. Or the victim may stage such a crime, report it to the police, and then file a fraudulent claim with their insurance company. It has become such a problem, that many insurance companies now employ investigators to detect fraudulent insurance claims.

We have had numerous reports involving people who were suspected of selling their vehicle for illegal narcotics. Often, the person will report that he or she was a victim of a car jacking and their vehicle was stolen during the car jacking. In some cases, the suspect wanted the drugs so bad, that they traded their vehicle for the illegal drugs. The suspect after making the transaction will begin to worry that his or her family and friends will discover their habit and attempt to figure out a way to replace their vehicle. That is when they invent the crime of the car jacking. They will report the vehicle as stolen and then file a claim with their insurance company. If the vehicle is not located within the allotted time reserved by the insurance company, the suspect will receive a check from the insurance company.

The drug suspect will either keep the vehicle or perhaps sell or trade the vehicle to someone else. After the vehicle is reported as stolen by the suspect claiming to be a victim of the car jacking, the vehicle is listed on the National Crime Information Center or NCIC. If an officer spots the vehicle, the driver of the vehicle will either attempt to evade capture and a car chase then occurs or the driver of the vehicle will obey the officer's request and be arrested for theft by receiving a stolen automobile. The driver of the vehicle may tell the officer, during or after the arrest that he or she purchased the vehicle from another person but they are unable to provide a bill of sale for the vehicle and have not attempted to register the vehicle in their name.

One fraud suspect under investigation for credit card skimming reported that he was the victim of a home invasion. The suspect told the responding police officers that someone knocked upon his door and when he answered the door, the perpetrators put a gun to his head. He said that the perpetrators then tied him with duck tape, stole some of his recording equipment, and his vehicle which was parked in the driveway. The fraud suspect told the police that the perpetrators kept asking him were the marijuana was. The fraud suspect attempted to let on that he didn't have any marijuana in the house and told the responding officers and detective that the perpetrators must have chosen the wrong location and got him mixed up with someone else.

I had been investigating the suspect for skimming credit cards and supplying those credit card numbers to another suspect of a larger Asian gang. He would have already been arrested for the credit card thefts but he had skimmed several credit cards at the restaurant that could not be linked back to him. The suspect had been listed as the server on about 90 percent of the compromised credit card numbers and the other 10 percent had been distributed among five other servers at the business. I suspected that the fraud suspect, during the restaurant's busiest times, completed the credit card transactions belonging to the other servers so that they could wait on other tables. When I questioned the other servers regarding the incident, they told me that they didn't ever let anyone else ring up the sale. Since the servers would not admit that they had broken the restaurant's operating procedures by allowing someone else to ring up their sales, I was left trying to piece together sufficient evidence to arrest and convict the fraud suspect. He could have been arrested and charged but I sincerely doubt I could have won the case in court. With the other servers names attached to several of the sales, it provided reasonable doubt for the suspect. I definitely needed more evidence on the suspect.

The fraud suspect filed an insurance claim with his insurance company a few days after the alleged home invasion. The suspect filed a claim reporting that the perpetrators had stolen about $35,000 in stereo and recording equipment and was attempting to have his insurance company pay for this loss. The insurance company's investigator became suspicious after obtaining the police report and discovering that the police report did not contain a lot of the items the suspect was claiming to have had stolen. The investigator began to question the claim and interview the suspect. After realizing that the investigator had alerted the police of the fraudulent claim, the suspect dropped the claim. I believe that this suspect was a gangster want-to- be and his association with other criminals led to the so called home invasion. This suspect will eventually slip up and make the mistake that will lead to his arrest. He may even face his demise by the hands of his associates. I know he was extremely lucky the night of the so-called home invasion because criminals that are attempting to recover their stolen funds or drugs will often maim and/or murder their associates to make a point.

Chapter Twenty-Seven

The Sleight of Hand Scam

Just about everyone has heard of or seen scams which contain some sleight of hand movements on the part of the fraud suspect. These can be of a variety of things such as loaded dice which always turn up a certain way, a card cheat capable of dealing cards he or she needs to win the hand, or in this case the swap. Hollywood has made a lot of movies which the story line had some type of confidence man or con man working the victim. One of my favorite movies, The Sting, was about a large scam. In the very first scene, three confidence men run a swap scam on another criminal. The great thing about that movie was that the scam was completed on another criminal. In the real world though, the victim is usually an innocent person that hasn't broken any laws and makes an honest living.

I remember one individual, years ago, came in to town. He asked if anyone wanted to bet on a card trick. The guy had three cards, each bent halfway in the middle. Two of the cards were Aces and the other one was a jack. For a $1.00, you could wager that you could pick the jack out of the three. If you were successful, he would pay you. If not, he kept your money. He would shuffle the three cards for several seconds and then place the cards, face down, in a row. A lot of people took the bet but no one was ever able to pick out the jack from the three cards. This guy left with about $100 of other people's money.

We had a couple of cases regarding con men running these sleight of hand cons. One case, in particular, found the victim discovering that the diamond she had for sale had been switched for a fake diamond. The victim had placed an advertisement in the classified section of the paper for the sale of a large diamond which she had. After placing the advertisement, the victim was contacted via telephone by someone with a thick African accent.

The suspect asked the victim several questions regarding the diamond's size, shape, and color. The suspect told the victim that he was interested in purchasing the diamond and a meeting was arranged at a local restaurant. The victim met the suspect at the restaurant. They sat at a table and the victim gave the diamond to the suspect. As the suspect was looking at the diamond, something occurred in the restaurant which created a diversion. As the victim looked away momentarily, the suspect switched the real diamond with a fake diamond. The fake diamond was pretty much the same color, size, and shape as the real diamond. After making the switch, the suspect told the victim that he had changed his mind and had decided that he didn't want to buy the diamond. The suspect gave the fake diamond to the victim and the two left the restaurant. Shortly after leaving the restaurant, the victim realized that the suspect had swapped her diamond for a fake diamond. She filed a police report that launched an investigation into the theft.

This victim, however, was not going to sit idly by. She decided that she would place another advertisement in the same paper regarding the sale of a similar diamond hoping that the suspect would take the bait. He did. When the suspect called the number listed in the advertisement, he asked the same questions that had been asked during the previous scam. If my memory serves me correctly, I believe that the victim had a friend answer the suspect's call. The victim, who had overheard the telephone conversation, was able to confirm that it was the same person with a thick African accent. Another meeting was scheduled with the suspect. Before this meeting, however, the Atlanta Police would stake out the location and wait for the suspect to arrive. The suspect came to the location and the victim positively identified him. The suspect was detained, identified, and arrested by the lead detective working the case. On his person was another counterfeit diamond. Although the victim did not recover her diamond, she was able to have the perpetrator arrested for the crime. All too often, the victim never receives their property back and the suspects are never identified or arrested.

There are several things to remember regarding this type of transaction. First, never let your guard down. Go in with the belief that this person could be attempting to rip you off. Second, never go to any such transaction by yourself. Bring a family member or close friend to help you. And third, never ever take your eyes off of your item.

Chapter Twenty-Eight

Civil vs. Criminal

Sometimes, cases can become quite complicated. Criminal cases can almost always be civil cases; however, civil cases cannot always be criminal. Often, a fine line exists between the two. For a case to proceed as criminal, some law must have been broken. These laws must be in effect and enacted by the state or federal legislature. For someone to be convicted of a criminal offense, the person must be found guilty beyond a reasonable doubt. Civil cases are cases when a person or persons believe that they have been wronged in one manner or another. A person or persons may bring a civil suit against another person or business for a lot of reasons. These reasons may vary from mental anguish, health reasons, injuries sustained from an accident, to wrongful death suits, etc. Civil suits are based on a preponderance of the evidence. Sometimes, a person may be found not guilty in a criminal trial and then have a civil judgment passed against them as in the high profile case in California a few years back.

Vehicle accidents, for example, are almost always of a civil nature. Chances are that an individual at fault in an accident will be cited for a violation and have to pay a fine. The person will not have to spend any time in jail unless other more severe circumstances exist such as driving under the influence, reckless driving, attempting to elude, driving a stolen vehicle, or driving on a license which has been served and surrendered, etc. Vehicle accidents are a leading cause of major injuries and deaths in the United States. Vehicle accidents usually occur because of someone's carelessness or stupidity and are seldom premeditated acts. A person at fault in a severe vehicle accident and his or her insurance company will more than likely be involved in a civil action.

Every so often, people will attempt to proceed criminally with something that is totally civil. It is the detective's and District Attorney's office that must decide if any laws have been broken before any investigation can proceed. Often a business partner who has lost money in a business venture will attempt to file criminal charges on the other partner or partners. If the detective or an Assistant District Attorney discovers that a law has been broken, then the case will proceed with an investigation. If not, the person or persons are advised that it is civil and that if they wish to proceed, should do so in Civil Court. Some people have attempted to bring criminal charges against an ex-friend and business partner when the business has failed and the friendship has gone sour. It is important to remember that our legal system cannot be used for revenge or retaliation but only for justice.

Many defense attorneys will make every attempt to convince the Court that the criminal case was not criminal, but civil, and should be dismissed. They attempt to "muddy the water", so to speak. Current trends in fraud related crimes have seen many fraud cases were the fraud suspect, under the guise of a legitimate business, began to steal from his or her clients or investors. The defense attorney will argue that it was an error or a mistake on his or her client's behalf and will produce evidence to show that their client did this or this correctly and this person or that person profited from the transactions. Mistakes and errors are part of everyday life. They are part of the learning process. I, personally, feel that if someone truly made an error or mistake, then that person will rectify the situation before it ever becomes criminal in nature. One word can be used to determine if the person actually stole and that is intent.

As an officer and later as a fraud detective, I made a lot of cases against individuals who had stolen from others or defrauded others. I made every attempt to gather all of the evidence that was available and build the best case. In my years, I only had a couple of cases dismissed or the suspect received a not guilty verdict.

One case, working with the U.S. Postal Inspector, was against an individual operating an investment and mortgage company. The suspect went to several churches in the Atlanta area and spoke with the congregations concerning investments and convinced them they could help their community and, at the same time, make a larger profit on their investment returns. Several people invested a great deal of money with this individual; many even refinanced their homes to obtain the funds needed for the investments.

Several women walked into the Major Fraud office to make a report on the suspect. One of the ladies had invested a substantial amount of funds with the suspect and had seen little or no return in her investment. The victim began to explain that the suspect had arranged for her to speak with a representative of a large investment firm and after speaking with the representative decided to withdraw her late husband's retirement funds and invest it with the investment firm of the representative. The victim received a check for the retirement funds which was made payable to the victim and investment firm for a rollover. After receiving the check, the victim gave the check to the suspect to send to the investment firm. The victim later found out that the check had not been deposited with the investment firm and contacted her late husband's company regarding the check. The victim retrieved a photocopy of the check from the institution. The photocopy of the check revealed that the check had not been deposited into an account at the intended financial institution but another institution in another state. The victim contacted this bank and discovered that the check had been deposited into an account bearing her name and that just about all of funds had been transferred to another account owned by the suspect. The suspect withdrew most of the funds from the account using an ATM card within the following months. It is uncertain as to how the suspect was able to deposit a check for such a large amount of currency in a banking institution on behalf of the victim when the check was made payable to the victim and another financial institution. I do have my suspicions though.

I obtained state arrest warrants and a search warrant for the suspect and his business. The suspect was arrested but was released at the preliminary hearing. The suspect's attorney was able to "muddy the water" by telling the judge that numerous others had benefited from the suspect's business and that the check in question was an error. Many things transpired that day that should not had. First, I was the only person called as a witness. The victim was told that she did not have to testify until a later date. I suppose that the D.A. felt, as I did, that we had enough to proceed. The evidence was at hand but the skillful defense attorney was very successful at convincing the judge that this case was civil and not criminal. I still disagree with that ruling and hope that justice finds its way to this lady and the others that this suspect defrauded.

Fraud cases can be very complicated in some instances. Under the guise of a legitimate business, suspects can commit fraudulent related crimes which are often very difficult to detect and investigate. I recommend that you are cautious with your investments. Take your time and investigate the person (s) or business. It may save you a lot of money and heartache down the road.

Some states have passed legislation regarding the writing and passing of worthless checks which, for one reason or another, were returned as being unpaid or stamped insufficient funds. In years past, some states had laws enacted that could enable law enforcement to exact an arrest on an individual if it could be proven that the person writing the check did not have the funds in their financial institution to cover the amount of the check. Since mistakes do happen and a lot of people do not keep their checking account balances accurately, most states now consider the writing and passing of a check more of a civil offense. When a person passes a check to another person or business and the check is labeled not payable or insufficient funds then the person or business can proceed by running the check through their financial institution again or if this does not resolve the matter, the person or business can initiate a demand letter. In Georgia, for instance, a person or business given a worthless check can attempt to recover their losses by instituting a demand letter.

The demand letter must be written in accordance with state law and usually requires the person's name, address, check number, banking institution, amount of the worthless check, and date of the worthless check be listed. The demand letter, in itself, demands payment of the worthless check within a certain number of days. The business or person may also impose a penalty. If the person does not comply with this demand letter within the time period, then the receiving party, person or business, may proceed criminally with the case. To proceed criminally on a deposit account fraud case, the receiving party must provide proof that the person writing the worthless check did, in fact, receive the demand letter or every attempt was made to locate that person but was unsuccessful. If the demand letter was received by the individual and the person or business has not received payment, the person or business can proceed with a criminal case.

The receiving party has two options at this point, they can apply for an arrest warrant for the individual, or they can turn the case over to law enforcement. I have investigated many cases of this type and a few suspects have made a career out of deposit account fraud. Some suspects have become so knowledgeable of state laws; they limit their checks to misdemeanor amounts. Some suspects even know what amounts will pass undetected by a store's security defenses and some even know certain tricks which enable the checks to pass without immediate detection.

One very important thing that businesses and persons receiving a worthless check should watch out for is that of identity theft or identity fraud. An identity fraud victim has their identity stolen and used by the suspect pretending to be the victim. The suspect will then obtain a counterfeit driver's license or identification card and if they have obtained the checking account information of the victim will then proceed to manufacture counterfeit checks. Since the checks contain the correct routing number of the victim's banking institution and the correct account number of the victim, the checks began to clear funds from the victim's account until no more funds are available. Checks that do not clear the account are returned to the business marked insufficient funds. The business then proceeds to attempt to collect those funds plus a penalty. This becomes a problem when the suspect or suspects have changed the address on the check to reflect another bogus address. The business will send a demand letter to the address on the check and, after the grace period, will attempt to proceed with the case criminally. It is extremely important that businesses investigate each incident thoroughly and completely to insure that the person who had written the worthless check was indeed that person and not a victim also. There have been many reports of an identity fraud victim being arrested for a crime that another perpetrator pretending to be the victim actually committed. Verification of such crimes can only be made by video surveillance evidence compared to actual photographs, latent fingerprints, or through a photographic lineup. I would not even contemplate an arrest warrant for an individual without any of the aforementioned three means of verification. Just because a person's name, address, or account number is on a check is not proof, in itself, to obtain an arrest warrant for that individual. There must be additional proof that the person responsible for passing the worthless instrument was, in fact, totally responsible for the criminal act.

Chapter Twenty-Nine

Fake Identification Cards

Often, a fraud perpetrator will need to obtain some type of identification if he or she is to be successful in their crimes. This is especially true with many forms of identity fraud, check fraud, and some credit card fraud or financial transaction card fraud. Since the fraud perpetrator does not want his or her true identity to be discovered and also to match the name, address, or other identifiers of the victim they will often purchase fake identification cards or driver's licenses that have their picture on the front of the card but have the personal information belonging to someone else, the victim.

These fake or counterfeit identification cards can range from a poor quality which can be detected by most people to those cards which have excellent quality. The fake identification cards with excellent features sometimes even give law enforcement trouble. Of course, this does cost the fraud perpetrator extra but some perpetrators are able to commit a larger number of crimes without being detected. Many states allow businesses to manufacture novelty identification cards intended for amusement purposes. People can have any name, address, and birth date applied to the novelty card. It may be of a super hero, cartoon character, or a famous person living or dead. Many states have regulations for these cards and usually have the word novelty imprinted on them using a specific style and size of lettering. A fraud perpetrator might purchase a novelty identification card and then remove the word novelty from the card. Some businesses which deal in this type of business have discovered that they can increase their earnings by secretly offering counterfeit identification cards under the table. The quality of the fake identification cards depends upon the expertise of the person making the card, materials, and photographic cameras. Some very experienced fraud perpetrators have begun to manufacture their own counterfeit cards by purchasing all of the necessary equipment. This way, they can quickly manufacture a counterfeit identification card to match any identity they have stolen.

The search of a fraud perpetrator after his or her arrest will often reveal a counterfeit identification card and sometimes, numerous counterfeit identification cards. These cards are seized as evidence of the crimes and often, the counterfeit identification cards used by these individuals in their crimes can be an essential part of a criminal case. The counterfeit identification card or a photocopy of a counterfeit identification card can be used by the District Attorney's Office as evidence that the person on trial was, indeed, the person that committed the criminal offense. We have had numerous cases where an unknown fraud perpetrator has committed fraudulent crimes using counterfeit identification cards with their picture upon the card and a stolen identity. Sooner or later, law enforcement will positively identify the suspect and then proceed to obtain arrest warrants for the suspect's criminal acts. This is especially true when the suspect purchases a new vehicle using a stolen identity. Dealerships will generally photocopy the identification card for their records especially if the suspect is obtaining financing through the dealership. These photocopies, depending upon their quality, can be used by law enforcement with other evidence to identify the fraud suspect and eventually exact an arrest.

I have had a couple of cases where the suspect possessed two driver's licenses issued by the state of Georgia. A search of the suspect after her arrest revealed the second driver's license. Each license contained the suspect's photograph; however, each license had a different name, address, and date of birth attached. After the arrest, I ran the first license the suspect had given me. It came back as being on file with no wants or warrants. At first, I thought that the second driver's license was an excellent counterfeit. I ran that license, and to my surprise, it came back as being on file with no wants or warrants. The suspect was advised of her Constitutional Rights and she agreed to speak with me without an attorney being present. When I questioned her about the second driver's license, she replied that her credit history was in shambles and that she had met a man in a bar who told her that he could repair her credit for a couple of hundred dollars. The suspect said that she later met the man again, gave him the money, and he gave her the paperwork which she used to obtain a new driver's license and open up new credit accounts. This information was passed along to the Department of Motor Vehicles for further investigation.

Sometimes, it is very difficult for business owners, managers, or employees to recognize a counterfeit identification card. There are several security measures known only to law enforcement and these measures cannot be given to the general public because if the fraud perpetrator has knowledge of these measures, they will soon defeat them. There are certain things that a business owner, manager, or employee can do to detect a counterfeit identification card. First take a good look at your own state issued driver's license or identification card. Often you can use the images of an authentic driver's license or identification card to identify a counterfeit identification card. One trick of fraud perpetrators is to present a counterfeit out-of-state identification card or driver's license. The fraud perpetrator knows that most business owners and employees will not know what a driver's license from another state looks like.

Chapter Thirty

Investigations

Investigations can be very complicated and time consuming. The general public often does not have any comprehension of what an investigation comprises. Television programs usually give the impression that investigations can be solved in little or no time without a whole lot of trouble. In real life, things are extremely different. A fraud investigation, for example, may take several months or years to investigate as the number of incidents and suspects magnify.

A typical fraud investigation may begin as a simple counterfeit check case or credit card fraud case. As the detective or investigator begins the investigation, he or she then begins to recognize aspects of the case which might resemble another case he or she has been assigned or recognize the modus operandi of an individual or criminal organization which depict the same criminal or organization. Often, the detective or investigator will discover that the fraud perpetrator has committed more and more crimes and that the fraud perpetrator has numerous accomplices which have perpetrated more and more similar crimes. Eventually, the detective or investigator is faced with an investigation that might include numerous perpetrators and several incidents.

Each incident needs to be investigated thoroughly. Interviews conducted, statements recorded, evidence retrieved, and reports written. The detective or investigator must be dedicated to the case and interview numerous victims and/or witnesses to each and every incident. Hours and hours of video surveillance must be reviewed, actual evidence retrieved such as that of a counterfeit check, fingerprint analysis left on recovered evidence, statements or affidavits of victims and witnesses, and a synopsis of the investigation completed. With just one incident, the time a fraud investigator spends may take several days or even weeks. If a fraud investigation reveals 40 or 50 perpetrators and several hundred incidents, the investigation may take several years before exacting an arrest of those criminally involved.

I know that, at one time, we had four detectives assigned to work fraud cases. The Major Fraud office received over 3,000 reports that year but not all could be investigated. Each detective, at that time, was working approximately 200 cases each. With this many cases each, a detective barely had time to investigate anything. It appeared that all of us were running around attempting to put out a fire here and then immediately go to another case to put that fire out. Sometimes, the detective had to drop every other case, for the time being, and concentrate on one huge case. Our way of thinking was that a huge case often involved several incidents and by clearing the huge case we could solve a lot of other smaller cases. Citizens actually had no idea of the volume of reports our office received each year and the enormous case load that each detective was assigned. I always felt bad for all of the victims especially those who lost a lot of time and money because of the fraudulent perpetrators. Every citizen, when they are a victim of a criminal act, should receive justice. A serious problem arises when there are so many incidents and too few detectives, investigators, or officers to investigate each and every one. Fraud detectives are extremely overworked and overwhelmed with the mass number of reports that come across their desk daily, weekly, monthly, and yearly. Most jurisdictions have but a handful of fraud detectives assigned to work financial crimes and fraudulent activity.

Fraud investigations do not receive the needed amount of manpower to adequately investigate all of the fraudulent criminal acts being committed within their jurisdiction. One reason, I believe, is because fraudulent activity is not classified as a Part One crime by the Federal Bureau of Investigation's Uniformed Crime Report or U.C.R. Although it is not intended to be used in such a way, Part One crimes on the U.C.R. are used by some to reflect the meanest and safest cities in the United States. The F.B.I. gathers information on eight Part One crimes: murder, robbery, rape, auto theft, larceny, burglary, aggravated assault, and arson. Fraudulent criminal acts are considered Part Two crimes. Jurisdictions report a loss or gain in criminal activity each year based on Part One crimes. Statistics are necessary to establish whether criminal acts are increasing or decreasing and may dictate what each jurisdiction needs to focus on. All too often, either through the media or other means, cities will focus on how they compare to other cities in the nation. Therefore, if a city is ranked in the top five cities in the nation as being unsafe then that city will probably make every effort to strengthen its police agency and direct their personnel in different ways to combat the rise in criminal behavior. Part Two crime records are also kept by the U.C.R. but are not given the attention of Part One crimes by police agencies.

Police agencies throughout the United States are faced with the enormous task of investigating the ever increasing number of fraud related crimes. The number of cases that a fraud detective or investigator is assigned will vary from jurisdiction to jurisdiction. Most of those that I have worked closely with were working between 50 and 200 cases at a time.

With such a large case load, the detective had to choose the case by severity. It was always difficult for me to try to explain to a victim who had their identity stolen by someone attempting to open a charge account in their name but, for one reason or another, was unsuccessful that their case probably would not get much attention. Now, don't get me wrong. It's not that I did not want to investigate the incident but it is very difficult to investigate an attempt of an identity fraud when you have over a hundred cases sitting on your desk where individuals and businesses have lost an enormous amount of money because the suspect(s) were successful.

Police agencies, throughout the nation, are often understaffed and do not have the adequate resources to combat criminal activities. Sometimes, police agencies are forced to minimize their force while, at the same time, provide the most service possible. Many citizens believe that an officer patrols the streets and neighborhoods preventing criminal behavior and apprehending those responsible. All too often, in a busy jurisdiction, the officer will bounce from 911 call to 911 call throughout his or her watch or shift. Sometimes, the officer has to make time to eat while driving to a call. Detectives and investigators of busy jurisdictions are often faced with an enormous case load and they attempt to investigate these cases the best they can. Some agencies have even incorporated thresholds for cases to be investigated. In other words, if the dollar loss of the victim or victims does not meet or exceed the threshold amount, the case will not be investigated by that agency or unit. The case is referred elsewhere.

If you are faced with this situation, do not give up hope, attempt to gather all the evidence that you can such as dates, times, and locations and request that businesses with video surveillance give you a copy or at least save a copy for the investigating jurisdiction.

Police agencies throughout the United States of America are not equipped to handle the mass volume of fraud related incidents which occur each year. Simply put, most jurisdictions do not employ enough detectives to investigate such cases or do not possess the necessary funds to combat such crimes. The more evidence a victim can provide will always be beneficial to the detective or investigator assigned to these fraudulent cases.

Chapter Thirty-One

Protecting Yourself

I do not believe that anyone can totally prevent becoming a victim of a fraudulent crime, such as identity fraud, but people can make it a whole lot harder for someone to use their personal information or financial information without their knowledge and consent. By taking certain steps, a person should be able to detect any fraud related activity and limit the amount of losses and headaches associated with the fraudulent criminal acts.

Suggestions:

- Check your banking accounts, credit card accounts, and any other financial accounts regularly, if not daily. Review the statements and all of the charges very closely. Many people only look at three things on a credit card statement: the balance, the minimum payment, and the due date. All too often, a skillful fraud perpetrator will use the account making only one or two purchases or withdrawals which they know have a chance of being undiscovered by the victim(s).

- Eliminate or limit the number of checks you write. Fraud perpetrators can cause you a lot of trouble if they obtain any of your account information. Have your personal checks sent to your banking institution or to a Post Office box. After receiving your checks, keep them in a safe place preferably a locked safe.

- Never place outgoing mail containing any personal or financial information in your mail box with the flag up. Always take this mail to a U.S. Postal facility and place the item(s) directly in a U.S. Postal mailbox. Keep watchful eyes in your neighborhood for people going through mail boxes. If you happen to see someone other than the postal employee or the home owner going through mail boxes, alert law enforcement and the United States Postal Inspections office immediately.

- Never give your P.I.N. or Personal Identification Number to any of your bank cards or credit cards to anyone. Never write you P.I.N. or Personal Identification Number on any of your bank cards or credit cards or keep your P.I.N. with your bank or credit cards. Memorize your P.I.N.

- If you have a personal computer or laptop, pay your bills through your financial institution's online banking system. This will enable you to make payments within 2 or 3 days and does not give anyone access to your banking account number. The number sent only references your account number and only you and the financial institution know who the reference number belongs to.

- Keep a watchful eye on your credit history. Often the credit report will reveal the first signs of identity fraud. Be especially watchful of the inquiries which have a reflection on your credit score or those inquiries which reveal that a credit application has been submitted. Many states offer a least one free credit report each year and some even offer two free reports per year. Some companies have enacted some type of credit watch for a monthly fee to help assist people in alerting them of fraudulent activity soon after it occurs.

- Keep your wallet on your person. Never place your wallet in your purse and place the purse by your desk. Never leave your purse or wallet, in plain view, inside of your vehicle. If placing the purse in the trunk of your vehicle, make sure no one is watching you do so. Never, ever, place your purse containing your wallet in a shopping cart while you are shopping. Fraud perpetrators will wait for the opportune time when you are concentrating elsewhere and then steal your purse or perhaps the wallet inside. Keep your purse close to you at all times.

- Limit the number of credit cards you carry on your person. You may also consider getting on a "don't send list" for credit card offers.

- Be extremely cautious of where you use your credit cards. Your card can be skimmed by someone such as a waiter or waitress. If possible, pay the bill with currency. If you do dine out a lot, I would recommend that you apply for a credit card just for that purpose. Request a low credit amount limit.

- Be cautious when using the World Wide Web or Internet. Never give your personal or financial information to anyone you do not know or trust. Be especially watchful for "phishing" emails. Never respond directly to any financial email by clicking reply. The page may look legitimate but often looks can be deceiving. Be safe by typing in the web address of the institution and reply through their customer service department. Never, never ever, give any personal or financial information on any email unless you know it is legitimate.

- If purchasing something from an online auction use a secure method to pay for the item or items. Never wire money or send a personal check as payment.

- Whenever using your personal computer or laptop computer, be certain that you have it protected with a quality security system and keep the system up to date.

- Do not carry your social security card or anything with your social security number on your person. Keep these in a safe place preferably a safe. If your driver's license or state identification card contains your social security number, have it removed immediately.

- Remember, good things often take a lot of hard work and time to accomplish. Get rich quick schemes are just that, schemes or cons the majority of the time. Few things in life have ever produced large dividends with a small amount of work. Be cautious and alert. Don't let your greed get the best of you. Always remember, if it sounds too good to be true it probably isn't true. Research and think before ever taking that first step. Never jump into anything without a lot of thought.

- Use whatever resources and organizations are available to research people and businesses before ever making a large investment. Thoroughly check the person and/or business out before ever turning over any of your hard earned money.

- Home owners thinking about remodeling or adding an addition to your home should research the contractor or sub contractors. Don't be afraid to ask questions and to ask for references. Talk with other home owners and look at the quality of work.

- Let the buyer beware. Be extremely cautious of whatever you are buying. Is it real or is it counterfeit. If it is a vehicle or a motorcycle, has the odometer been rolled back to reflect a lower mileage? Has it been damaged and then repaired? Is it a stolen item?

- Let the seller beware also. Fraud perpetrators have used various methods to defraud someone or a business of their items or merchandise. Be cautious when accepting payments such as personal checks, payroll checks, and cashier's checks. Many fraud perpetrators will attempt to pass off a counterfeit cashier's check at a time when banks are closed for business. If you are accepting a check for a large amount of money, be certain to do so when you can verify the check at a banking facility.

- Learn about fraudulent activities. The more that you know, the less likely you are to become a victim. Fraud perpetrators will often use schemes and scams which another perpetrator has taught them. Some things will change but the overall scheme remains about the same. There is a world of knowledge that can be obtained by simply doing a little research.

- Be especially careful when using an ATM or Automated Teller Machine. Make sure that the area is free of obstructions which could be hiding a robbery perpetrator. Also, become acquainted with the ATM that you use regularly. Look carefully at the card insert slot. Skillful credit card skimmers can fabricate skimming devices which appear to be part of the ATM. These skimming devices will protrude from the card insert slot and are held to the machine by double sided tape. If you notice that the ATMs appearance is different than usual, contact the bank's security department or law enforcement agency and report the incident. Always try to use the ATM in a secure environment and if someone quickly approaches you, remain calm and be certain to remove your currency and your card from the machine.

- Protect and safeguard your personal identifiers and your financial information. Keep them in a safe place preferably a safe deposit box or perhaps a small secured home or business safe. Do not dispose of papers containing any such information without shredding them first. Request that your employer, doctor(s), dentist, and anyone else having your information safeguard it just as you. On a special note to business owners and managers, take extra precautions to safeguard the personal and financial information of your clients and employees. All businesses should keep these records locked away, preferably in a locked safe. Old records containing personal and financial identifiers should be destroyed by fire or by shredding. Under no circumstance should these records be thrown into a dumpster or placed in a storage area. Be extremely careful about giving any information to someone via the telephone. Fraud perpetrators have been known to contact the victims pretending to be a representative for a legitimate business and request that the victims update their personal and/or financial information. Incidents have also occurred when individuals have made payments via the telephone. The victim willfully submits their account information, credit card, or checking account, to the business' representative. The representative of the business will copy the information on a piece of paper and later that day leaves the business with the victim's financial and/or personal identifiers.

- Last, but not least, always keep your guard up and be alert. By taking a few simple steps, precautions, and gaining knowledge of fraudulent activities and criminal acts you can prevent or deter a lot of stress, heartache, and losses.

If you become a victim, file a police report. If several crimes occur in several different jurisdictions, attempt to file a police report with each jurisdiction. Contact the stores or businesses and speak to the loss prevention manager or store manager regarding saving the video surveillance footage for law enforcement. If you become a victim of identity fraud, file reports or complaints with the Federal Trade Commission, FTC, and the National White Collar Crime Center, NW3C, in addition to police reports. Attempt to compile as much information about the criminal incident as possible. Attempt to locate the exact location where the suspect or suspects committed the criminal incidents. Large chain stores usually have a numbered system to identify the location of the store. The customer service department or asset protection department should be able to advise you of the store's location. A financial institution can advise you of the location of a particular branch.

In addition, to the aforementioned paragraph, victims also need to:

- File Affidavits of Fraud or Forgery with each creditor or business for all incidents.

- Maintain a log of activity i.e. telephone calls, letters, and office visits etc.

- Obtain a complete history of the account for the investigation.

- Send the creditor a letter pursuant to FCRA 609e so that law enforcement can begin the investigation quicker without a subpoena for the production of evidence.

- Place a fraud alert on your credit history with one of the three major credit bureaus and then place an extended fraud alert thereafter.

- Check your criminal history and motor vehicle driver's history.

- Check with the Social Security Office yearly to receive a copy of yearly earnings and withholdings.

- Contact your Representative and Senator regarding changes in the Law and Credit Acts.

Many fraud cases cannot be solved to the extent of an arrest of the fraud perpetrator or perpetrators. Sometimes, the evidence needed is incomplete or perhaps the evidence is just too circumstantial. Time is a definite factor in a lot of cases. The quicker evidence is obtained and organized, the better chance the case has for being solved. It is difficult to solve a case, such as an identity fraud, when several months or years have passed. Much of the evidence has either been destroyed or lost and what is left usually is not enough for law enforcement to exact an arrest of the suspect.

There is an old saying in sports, "Offense wins games, but defense wins championships". The more knowledgeable you are concerning fraudulent activities and the more alert you are, the less likely you are to become a victim.

ACKNOWLEDGEMENTS

I would like to take this opportunity to thank all of the law enforcement agencies, courts, and corporate security throughout this great nation of ours for their fight against fraudulent crimes. I would also like to thank the following agencies for their tremendous effort in the ongoing fight against fraudulent crimes: the Federal Trade Commission, the National White Collar Crime Center, the Federal Bureau of Investigation, the United States Postal Inspections, the Governor's Office of Consumer Affairs, the Georgia State Attorney's General Office, the State Bar of Georgia, Georgia Department of Banking and Finance, the United States Immigration and Customs Enforcement, and the Attorney for the United States of America. I would especially like to thank the Atlanta Police Department and the United States Secret Service. It has been an honor and a privilege to have known and worked with such fine men and women of honesty, character, and integrity.